MW01252756

BEING THE CHOSEN

For Anna who is love and faith
For Millie who is love and hope

Being the Chosen
Exploring a Christian Fundamentalist Worldview

JULIE SCOTT JONES
Manchester Metropolitan University, UK

ASHGATE

Published by
Ashgate Publishing Limited
Wey Court East
Union Road
Farnham
Surrey, GU9 7PT
England

Ashgate Publishing Company
Suite 420
101 Cherry Street
Burlington
VT 05401-4405
USA

www.ashgate.com

British Library Cataloguing in Publication Data
Scott Jones, Julie.
  Being the chosen : exploring a Christian fundamentalist
  worldview.
  1. Fundamentalism--United States. 2. Fundamentalists--
  United States.
  I. Title
  280.4'0973-dc22

Library of Congress Cataloging-in-Publication Data
Jones, Julie Scott, 1966-
  Being the chosen : exploring a Christian fundamentalist worldview / by Julie Scott Jones.
    p. cm.
  Includes bibliographical references and index.
  ISBN 978-0-7546-7741-3 (hardback) -- ISBN 978-0-7546-9472-4 (ebook)
 1. Fundamentalism--United States. 2. Protestantism--United States. 3. United States--
Church history. 4. Christianity--Philosophy. I. Title.

  BT82.2.J65 2010
  230'.04626--dc22

                                                        2010007199

ISBN   9780754677413 (hbk)
ISBN   9780754694724 (ebk)

Mixed Sources
Product group from well-managed
forests and other controlled sources
www.fsc.org Cert no. SGS-COC-2482
© 1996 Forest Stewardship Council
FSC

Printed and bound in Great Britain by
TJ International Ltd, Padstow, Cornwall

Contents

Preface

To say this book, or at least a version of it, is a long time coming would be an understatement; it has been a decade in the writing. It has taken me a long time to process the fieldwork experience that I had at God's Way[1] religious community; the 'Chosen' whose worldview was the catalyst for and is the central focus of this book. Things also invariably get in the way of writing: teaching, family, and other commitments.

When I did my fieldwork in the USA, fundamentalism was viewed stereotypically as 'backward', 'retreatist' and 'anti-modern'; something of a relic and a peculiarity of American Protestantism. It was not a subject of much interest beyond a subdivision of the sociology of religion. Even Islamic fundamentalism was understudied and again rarely beyond the confines of specialist religious research. Following the events of 9/11, things have changed in how we view what was once described as 'extreme' religion: the need to engage with and more importantly to understand religious fundamentalism is a key issue of our time and should be a necessary component of any socio-political and economic policy making.

This book has two central aims; firstly to outline and explain the nature of a Protestant fundamentalist worldview. The second aim is to account for fundamentalist agency and action in the world, which is informed and shaped by this worldview. Ultimately, the aim is 'understanding' in its broadest sense; this book argues that one cannot understand and thus engage with fundamentalist movements and groups unless one understands the subtle interplay between worldview and action. The book draws on my participant observation based, ethnographic field research, living among a group of Protestant fundamentalists ('God's Way' community) to illustrate its central points.

The book that I would have written 'fresh' from fieldwork would have looked very different and would have been a more conventional ethnographic account. My understanding of God's Way, and fundamentalism more generally, has evolved over time and I am glad that I have chosen to write now. This book is not a textbook but it is written for my students. I have taught successive classes of sociologists of religion since 1996, every class has taught me something. You will never know how much I am indebted to you for making me think through my work, for embracing 'astonishment', for sharing ideas and viewpoints; as well as pushing me to be a better teacher. This book is for you all.

Julie Scott Jones, 2010

---

1 A pseudonym.

Acknowledgements

I would like to thank the Department of Sociology at Manchester Metropolitan University for support during the production of this book. I would like to thank Neil Jordan, my commissioning editor at Ashgate, for his support and assistance during the writing and production of this book; as well as the rest of his editorial team.

Chapter 1

'Furiously Religious': Contextualising Fundamentalism

Religious Fundamentalism … the Exception to the Theory

Religious fundamentalism has been a subject for research since the 1920s (Barr, 1977, Marsden, 1980). Initially research focused on fundamentalism among American Protestants, for reasons that will be discussed in Chapter 3 of this book. This early research focused initially on theological issues, such as, fundamentalists' reaction to the rise in Biblical criticism, secularism, theological liberalism, and the teaching of evolutionary theory in schools (Ammerman, 1993, Marsden, 1980). As well as exploring the interconnections between fundamentalists, evangelicals and other charismatic and traditional Protestant churches.

Sociologists of religion became interested in American Protestant fundamentalists, as they did not 'fit' neatly into sociology's central dogma: the secularisation thesis (Ammerman, 1993). This group of inter-related theories have dominated sociological accounts of religion's (particularly Christianity's) position in relation to modernity. It contends, to put it simply, that as society modernises religion 'loses its social significance' (Wilson, 1966) and becomes a matter for private choice or conscience. Religion as a socio-political or economic institution with a key structural role within society (as was the case in pre-modern European societies) is dismantled, eroded and eventually ceases (Bruce, 2002). Mainstream religion is then left to become a provider of life-cycle (for example, naming, marriage, and funeral rituals) and calendrical rituals (for example, harvest festivals, Christmas, and Easter), which become increasingly secularised (Bruce, 2002). It may serve as an historical 'memory' resource (Hervieu-Leger, 2000) that communities can draw upon to reinforce a sense of shared identity based on perceived past patterns of beliefs. Religion can become an identity provider for marginalised communities, such as migrant communities (Herberg, 1956, Bruce, 2002). Finally, religion operates as a meaning 'safety net' to be used when mainstream meaning systems, such as science or medicine appear to 'fail' to resolve individual or communal existential 'worries' (Davie, 1994, Berger, 1967). Religion shifts from a communal activity, at the heart of social life, with a key role in reinforcing social norms and consensus to a matter of individual 'choice' (Bruce, 2002, Heelas, 1997). Thus, religion becomes 'privatised' and a matter of consumer 'choice', which is demonstrated, in western societies, by the popularity of New Age beliefs with their focus on self-sacralisation and an 'if it works for you, it works' ethos (Heelas, 1997). It can also be seen in the phenomenon of 'believing without belonging' where people still appear to believe or have some sense of attachment to the idea of believing but choose not to attend regularly an actual place of worship (Davie, 1994). The gap between statistics which show low church attendance rates but relatively high (65 to 75 per cent) rates for belief in god/spirit (Davie, 1994, Bruce, 2002) also suggest 'privatisation' and individualised spirituality at work.

In many respects, mainstream religion (specifically Christianity) in the western context is following the wider social trend for a structural division between 'public' and 'private' domains. This divide is not present in pre-modern societies: moral issues, family life, personal conduct, work, and so forth are conducted in 'public' and open to scrutiny and communal monitoring; hence the high levels of cohesion and control in such societies (Foucault, 1979). Modernisation brings with it structural changes that create a divide between the 'public' spheres of work, social participation, social institutions, etc. and the 'private' sphere of family, sexuality, individual conduct, etc. An example of this is how the state retracts from moralising, monitoring, and interfering in private matters such as family life and sexuality: only becoming involved in matters of child protection and public decency (Sennett, 1996).

Fundamentalism among American Protestants challenged the secularisation thesis' account of religion and modernity in the western context (Ammerman, 1993). Fundamentalists do not recognise a division between the 'public' and 'private'; God is everywhere and thus everything is under scrutiny, nothing is 'private'. Similarly, faith is not for them a matter of individual, consumer 'choice' but rather a 'gift' bestowed on them by God. Most important of all is that God and faith should be at the heart of society and embedded within all society's structures and institutions (Ammerman, 1991, Bruce, 2008). Therefore, while the majority of western European societies appeared to follow the secularisation model in respect to Christianity; Christianity in America and particularly in relation to the phenomenon of fundamentalism posed a theoretical quandary. Initially theorists explained the emergence of American Protestant fundamentalism as a 'knee jerk' reaction to modernisation: a retreatist position taken by communities who could not 'cope' with the modern and more importantly secular world (Ammerman, 1993). This was a 'neat' theoretical account in that it explained away the fact that fundamentalism had emerged in the most modern of modern societies: the USA. It also reinforced the stereotype that is implied subtly within secularisation theories that religious people are somehow 'backward', 'irrational' and 'anti-modern'. This theoretical account of fundamentalism remained dominant until the 1980s; it was reinforced by the seeming lack of fundamentalism elsewhere in the world. In other words, this seemed like a peculiarity of American Protestantism. Additionally, American Protestant fundamentalism did not seem to be anything other than a regressive theological movement. However, this perception started to change in the late 1970s with two events that caused researchers to think again about religious fundamentalism (Ammerman, 1993, Bruce, 2008).

In 1976, President Jimmy Carter, who claimed to be a 'born-again' Christian, was elected, in part, by the mobilisation of evangelical and fundamentalist Protestant voters. Yet, Carter's politics and actions while president did not demonstrate any specific allegiance to this bloc grouping; nor did he enact legislation to change the relationship between church and state. Religion and religious-moral issues were not central preoccupations of his administration, despite his professed personal beliefs. However, his election did bring this brand of conservative Protestantism into public consciousness at a national and global level. In 1979, evangelical and fundamentalist churches, groups and communities mobilised against Carter and campaigned for future President Ronald Reagan, who was elected in 1980. Reagan, unlike Carter, openly courted this bloc of voters (and raised important campaign funds in the process) and campaigned on some issues, such as abortion, which were central to evangelical and fundamentalist campaigns. The rise in political influence, both as fundraisers and agenda setters, of evangelical and fundamentalist Protestants caught Americans 'by surprise' (Ammerman 1993: 1). The extent to which Reagan, when in power, actually placed evangelical and fundamentalist concerns at the heart of his administration, is open to debate (Bruce, 1990). The importance rather is that by the 1980s this bloc of Protestants had become a political and culturally influential group who could not be ignored. The reasons behind the emergence and rise of American Protestants, as well as the differences between evangelicals and fundamentalists will be explored in Chapters 2 and 3 of this book.

In 1979 another event happened that raised awareness of and changed how we think about so-called 'fundamentalists': the Iranian revolution. The Iranian leader Shah Mohammed Reza Pahlavi was overthrown in February 1979, by the religico-political movement led by the Ayatollah Ruhollah Khomeini. Khomeini had become a focus for Iranians' disaffection with the socio-economic consequences of the Shah's 'White Revolution' of the 1960s, which had at its heart an agenda of modernisation (including industrialisation and urbanisation) and ideological westernisation (including encouraging a consumer society, asserting secular values, eradicating gender divides, encouraging western style dress and 'tastes'). The 'Shah's Revolution' had created a prosperous urban middle class, but the majority of working class Iranians remained poor and excluded from the benefits of the consumer society built on Iran's oil economy. The Shah's increasingly repressive regime also facilitated dissent among Iran's urban poor. The mosques soon became the focus of dissent. Ayatollah Ruhollah Khomeini became the figurehead of the revolutionary movement, despite being in exile in France (Salehi, 1998, Daniel, 2001).

Khomeini reasserted the need for an Islamic government, what he called 'God's Government', essentially a theocracy ruled by ultra-conservative Islamic clerics, who stressed a literal interpretation of Islam and the dismantling of all things secular, western and 'unIslamic' that the Shah had established (Salehi, 1998, Daniel, 2001). The Iranian revolution had been fermenting for many years but the new regime again proved surprising for political commentators and researchers of religion alike. Again, the secularisation thesis proves inadequate in accounting for modernisation's impact on religion, in this instance Islam. It was presumed that the European model of modernisation, which has secularisation as a key consequence, would be applicable elsewhere in the world, irrespective of the religion in question. More importantly, the Iranian Revolution popularised the word 'fundamentalism'.

Although, as will be discussed in Chapter 2, the word 'fundamentalism' has its roots in early twentieth century American Protestantism; it was not used beyond theological or sociological circles. Following the events in Tehran in 1979, the word entered mainstream usage as the media adopted it to describe the new Islamic republic's version of Islam, in an attempt to offer a simplistic description of it for a western audience with little or no knowledge of any variety of Islam. From this point onwards, the term 'fundamentalism' would be used to refer to extremism and politicisation in all varieties of religion (Scott Jones, 2009). It became a word, which slowly drifted from its theological origins within American Protestantism (Scott Jones, 2009). Increasingly, 'fundamentalism' has become a pejorative label, often used synonymously with 'terrorism', which is one reason that many theorists avoid using the term at all (Munson, 1995). This issue will be explored in greater depth in Chapter 2. Iran remains, since the fall of the Taliban who ruled Afghanistan from 1996 to 2001, the world's only example of a long-standing fundamentalist state.

By the 1980s 'fundamentalism' has entered a wider public consciousness where it would remain through the long standing 'culture wars' in the USA in the 1980s and 1990s; and in the powerful political movements that would support successive Bush administrations and rally support against the Clinton and more recently Obama administrations. The rise of Islamic fundamentalism, beyond the continuing existence of the Iranian version, and its ties to radicalisation and in some instances terrorism, further illustrates the power of religious fundamentalism. Within the social sciences, particularly sociology, fundamentalism has proven to be a key element in critiques of the secularisation thesis, proving as Peter Berger puts it that the modern world is 'as furiously religious as ever' (1999, 2). Challenges to the secularisation model have now rightly seen it revised as a model almost exclusive to Europe and her satellites (Bruce, 2002). Fundamentalism also remains the best example of what happens when religious communities become politicised and the role that religious beliefs can play in political activity. Religion can be a powerful revolutionary force, as exemplified by the Iranian example.

The Extent of Religious Fundamentalism

Fundamentalism occurs in all the world's major religions, including Christianity, Islam, Judaism, Hinduism and Buddhism. Marty and Appleby's five volume 'Fundamentalism Project' (1991–1995) illustrates the diversity and spread of religious fundamentalism across the world's religions and regions. As fundamentalism is a theological term this should be expected; it should exist in all religions in the same way that 'liberalism', 'conservatism' and so forth, also exist. However, as will be discussed in the next chapter, 'fundamentalism' is also a sociological label that implies a specific worldview and an element of politicisation, usually leading to socio-political action in the world. Although fundamentalism can be found in all the major religions of the world, it predominates in the monotheistic, religions of 'the book', i.e. Judaism, Christianity, and Islam (Marty and Appleby, 1991, Bruce, 2008). This is not surprising given fundamentalism's focus on scriptural literalism and claims to a unifying and single 'true' reality. Fundamentalism is less likely to prosper in religions with less focus on one single authoritative account of 'reality, i.e. a central sacred scripture, and a unitary view of god. Therefore it is no surprise that fundamentalism predominates in Christianity (particularly Protestant varieties) and Islam.

Although fundamentalism can be located throughout the world's faiths and across the globe it is difficult to accurately chart the size of fundamentalist populations. One reason for this is definitional (Ammerman, 1993, Scott Jones, 2009): the term 'fundamentalist' is not often used by so-called 'fundamentalists', they prefer to adopt names that stress their mission or uniqueness, such as 'God's soldiers' or 'God's Way'. The over-use of the term in a pejorative sense also lumps non-fundamentalists together with 'actual' fundamentalists; too often traditionalists, the orthodox, and conservatives are lumped together and mislabelled as 'fundamentalists'. The latter is particularly a problem when looking at Islam, which stresses orthodoxy (the right way to believe) and orthopraxy (the right way to act or behave), as core tenets; often leading to traditional or conservative Muslims being categorised as fundamentalists (Scott Jones, 2009). Generally, it could be said that fundamentalism is widespread across the Islamic world, particularly, where modernisation (and westernisation) have created socio-economic inequalities and marginalised communities; for example, in Egypt, Iraq, Turkey, Indonesia and Malaysia. Jewish fundamentalism is an active agent in stalling and fuelling the Israeli-Palestinian conflict. Within Christianity, Protestant fundamentalism is growing in influence in South America, some parts of Europe and remains a significant force in the USA (Scott Jones, 2009). The final chapter of this book will explore the extent of religious fundamentalism on a global scale and explores some of the reasons for fundamentalism's continued growth.

A Way of Viewing the World

This book is about Protestant fundamentalism in the USA, although it will look at the wider global context of fundamentalism in the final chapter, Chapter 9. The book explores Protestant fundamentalism through looking specifically at the fundamentalist worldview. As was noted previously, fundamentalism is a theological label for a particular approach to religion, but it is also a socio-political term that stresses agency and political activity in the secular world. Fundamentalists were once stereotyped as 'retreatist and 'anti-modern' but rather than retreat back into literal, 'blind faith', these are individuals and more importantly communities that seek to act in the world; to effect change. They do not retreat from the modern world but rather offer an alternative version of modernity, which places religion at its heart. In doing so, they also posit a powerful critique of modernity. Fundamentalists may have an end goal that is otherworldly (for example, to enter heaven or survive the end of the world), but in the interim, they seek to effect socio-political change in the present. They willingly utilise the 'modern' against itself, for example, making extensive use of modern media technology, such as the Internet and satellite television, to disseminate their beliefs and mobilise communities (Marty and Appleby, 1991). However, action and a blueprint for social change and political action can only be understood through locating such action within an individual or community's worldview.

A worldview is, simplistically, how individuals see, understand and interpret the world around them (Gerth and Mills,1991). Everyone in that sense has a worldview; we all see the world in a subjective way that is unique to us. However, as Berger and Luckmann (1966) note, it is more complex than that. Our worldview is an all encompassing, 'comprehensive meaning system' that establishes what is 'social reality'; why 'social reality' is how it is; and it also accounts for why 'social reality' may change (Berger and Luckmann, 1966). In that sense worldviews are normative and explanatory (Berger, 1967, Berger and Luckmann, 1966); they establish 'the norm' and account for it. To illustrate, we agree the sky is blue and not green, and we can offer an explanation for it. To suggest the sky is not blue is to then go against a shared consensus, which is presented as 'commonsense'. Worldviews are built on and maintained by meaning systems, that is, forms of knowledge by which 'reality' is established. Meaning systems are typically built on one default form of knowledge; for example, in most modern societies scientific, empirical knowledge is the default (Berger and Luckmann, 1966). To illustrate, one would not got to the exorcist if one fell ill; one would seek out medical assistance and remedies, based on empirically tested knowledge that we can 'prove' works, for example, taking antibiotics to cure an infection. Meaning systems (and therefore worldviews) change and thus so do the knowledge forms on which they are built (Berger and Luckmann, 1966). Consider the reaction of an individual in the Middle Ages when confronted with what we today would label as 'epilepsy': it would have been explained as demonic possession and the expected, i.e. 'normal' thing to do would have been to call for an exorcist. Such action today would be seen as 'irrational' and 'odd'. Although most meaning systems are built on a default knowledge position, individuals and communities' worldviews may shift and draw on alternative knowledge providers in the face of the failure of the dominant meaning system (and knowledge) to account for reality. For example, if an individual remained seriously ill, despite the best efforts of modern, western medicine, she may be drawn towards a religious knowledge base instead. 'Moral panics' (Cohen, 1972) are a good example of how communities can shift their meaning-knowledge position in the face of seeming disruption to their 'social reality'. Although we have individual worldviews that are subjective; society requires some semblance of consensus on what is 'really real'. If we fail to have consensus on what is 'real' then existential chaos threatens and we begin to appreciate that what is 'real' is a mere social construction; at that stage 'anomie' becomes a reality and society may become chaotic. Thus, socialisation operates to socialise individuals with regard to what the group agrees is 'reality' (Berger and Luckmann, 1966). The accepted version of 'reality' is hegemonic, and maintained and reinforced by society's key social structures and through forms of control. Psychology (for example, the Asch conformity experiments of the 1950s) has long demonstrated the innate human tendency to conform to the group consensus, even if the individual believes the group's interpretation to be wrong. Thus, worldviews may have a subjective aspect: we have agency to act in the world and interpret to what extent we adhere to the hegemonic version of reality (Berger and Luckmann, 1966). Nevertheless, worldviews are built upon shared understandings of what is 'reality'.

Religious based meaning systems are particularly powerful providers of 'social reality', partly because they solve the issue of 'meaning crisis' far better than alternative knowledge forms. Weber (1991) labelled humanity's self-consciousness a 'curse' because it meant that we search for meaning to our existence. The majority of us are not content to accept that we live in an arbitrary and random universe, where to put it colloquially, 'shit happens'. We want, again to put it colloquially, 'shit to happen for a reason'. Most of modern, western life is secure and the sorts of events that forced individuals and communities in the past to confront the discrepancy between how reality should look and how it actually is no longer trouble us; for example, famine, natural disasters, plague etc. However although our lives are safer and more sanitised we still have what Weber (1991) called the 'meaning problem'. That is there remain the big existential questions of existence; they may not trouble us on an everyday basis but at different stages of the life course they challenge us for an answer. The 'why are we here', 'where are we going', 'what happens when I die', 'why get up in the morning to do the same thing I did yesterday and the day before', and so forth, are questions that need an answer. Our default empirical-scientific meaning system is not very effective in offering an answer that emphasises human significance. Consider, 'you are here because of billions of years of evolution' makes humans appear (and rightly so) rather insignificant in the wider scheme of things. As does the notion that 'when you die you become worm food'. Religious meaning systems offer answers that place humanity at their centre and make people (and their actions) seem significant and that they have a greater destiny beyond the often mundane everydayness of life; for example, 'you are a gift from God' and 'when you die, you might go to heaven'. Additionally, religious meaning systems are more effective in times of individual and communal 'meaning crises'. Geertz (1966) identifies three key categories of events that have the potential to create 'meaning crisis': the problem of evil (i.e. why do bad things happen to good people; why do bad people prosper), suffering (i.e. if there is a God why is there disease, pain, tragedy, etc) and bafflement (i.e. when events occur or phenomena are viewed that cannot be placed in the accepted interpretative framework). Scientific or secular meaning systems may explain 'evil' through psycho-pathology or neurology, for example, that an individual's brain chemistry or inadequate parenting while young, makes them a dangerous psychopath. Suffering can be accounted for through medicine or psychology, for example, you have a gene for cancer or your child died because they have caught a particular virus. Baffling events can be explained away as hallucinations, inventions and superstitions. Again these fail to offer a 'why me' account of why am I a victim of evil or suffering or have experienced bafflement. Religious meaning systems use characters such as 'the Devil' to account for evil or beliefs such as 'possession'. Suffering can be explained away through concepts such as 'sin', 'karma' or by 'god's will'. Bafflement can be accounted for through belief in magical or spiritual beings, such as Jinns or ghosts, or through the view that 'God works in mysterious ways'. 'Meaning crisis' develops when a gap emerges between how 'social reality' is perceived through lived experience and how people believe it should actually be. As Weber (1991) and Berger and Luckman (1966) all note, the majority of us cannot live in a state of meaninglessness. If we did, we would see 'reality' for what it is; a human construction, open to change. To confront this issue would cause 'meaning crisis', or what Durkheim (1989) called 'anomie'. Societies cannot function effectively when 'anomic'; they need to have a shared view of reality. Simplistically, imagine if we all had a different view of the colour of the sky; consensus is fundamental for societies to function.

Religious worldviews are so powerful because they draw on knowledge that appears to offer the 'whole story' and their power is supported by three key mechanisms: legitimations (Berger, 1967), such as sacred scriptures, that explain the how and why of reality. For example, the Bible offers an account of why we are here; how we should conduct ourselves while here; and what happens when we die and when/how the world will end. Legitimations can offer powerful explanations as to reality and are hard to criticise and challenge as to do so would be to literally 'take on' God. For example, the European feudal system or the Indian caste system were predicated on a view that this was a 'god given' social hierarchy and that one's place was decreed by God himself. Such legitimations are used to socialise the next generation of believers into the shared view of reality. The effectiveness of socialisation, particularly primary socialisation, has been well documented (Berger and Luckmann, 1966). Few of us stray from the belief systems with which we were socialised as children. This is also one of the reasons why religions focus so much on issues of family and education. They appreciate that socialising the next generation is crucial for their long-term survival. Finally, mystificatory devices (Berger, 1967), such as rituals, are used to 'mystify' beliefs by removing the 'hand of man' and thus supporting the view of 'reality' as God given. Mystification also focuses people's attentions on instrumental activities such as rituals and away from questioning 'reality'. Other meaning systems lack such a repertoire, which is partly one of the reasons why even in modern societies religion has not died out, as was once predicted and anticipated. Therefore, an exploration of how believers view and build reality is the key to understanding other aspects of their lives, beliefs, and activities.

This book's central focus is on outlining and exploring some key components of the worldview of Protestant fundamentalists and indeed religious fundamentalists in general. It does this by drawing predominantly from one specific case study of American Protestant fundamentalism: 'God's Way'[1] community.

Introducing 'God's Way' Community

I conducted long-term, participant observation, ethnographic research in God's Way community (Scott, 1996). I lived as a member of the group for just under a year. God's Way community consist of thirty-seven individuals who believe that they are uniquely 'chosen' by God as 'his people' to do 'his bidding'. The community was originally founded by their charismatic leader, 'Abraham Zion'[2] in 1927 in Arizona. However, following a series of natural disasters that the community interpreted as a series of punishments and 'tests' from God, the community migrated to southern Missouri where the present day community was established in April 1935. Abraham had been 'called' by God, via a series of dreams, to found the community and gather followers. In 1939, he experienced a series of powerful visions where God 'spoke' to him and dictated a new 'version' of the Bible. These scriptures were written-up and are called the 'Books of Abraham'. They play a central role in communal worship and complement their study of the Bible. They view the Bible as the product of centuries of 'editing' and 'rewriting' by the 'enemies of God', specifically, Catholics. Therefore, they use the Bible as a secondary source in relation to their own communal scripture. Both texts are taken literally as guides for living and a source of advice on all matters of faith.

The community established their current day ranch and built up a prosperous farm. During the post-war years they experienced a period of growth and the community's population peaked. Although initially isolationist, as they prospered they became more open to 'outsiders' and worked alongside local church groups who shared some of their beliefs. However some members became disaffected with this networking on common interests, as well as the increasing problem with the community's youth becoming influenced by the 1960s 'youth culture'. By the late 1960s, Abraham's health had deteriorated to such an extent that the issue of succession needed to be resolved. This issue became a focal point for increasing communal tensions around the future direction and aims of the community, particularly around external engagement and action. Isaac and Joshua are the two eldest sons of Abraham and by 1973, the community had split into two factions, each led by one of the sons. This conflict came to a head with a schism and Joshua led one half of the community away to found a rival group, which stressed a more literal, 'basic' way of life, without any use of modern technology or comforts. On departure, this group deliberately set fire to the community's buildings, destroying

---

1   A pseudonym.
2   All community members' names are pseudonyms.

most of the community's infrastructure and killing several members. Isaac assumed leadership of what remained of God's Way; a role that was formalised following the death of his father. Rebuilding following the fire is still ongoing and the community exists on a subsistence level on their ranch; they rely on work as contract labourers for local farmers to supplement their income. The community try to balance self-sufficiency and isolation with the need to participate in the 'outside' world for economic reasons. Isaac interpreted the fire and his father's death as divine 'punishment' for opening up the community to 'outside' influences and so the group attempt to maintain an isolationist stance. How successful this is will be discussed in later chapters.

The community's isolation has meant that few new members have been recruited, bar one family and they face a growing demographic issue, whereby nearly all the members are related either through birth or marriage and therefore the younger generation will struggle to find spouses within the group. This may force the community to recruit more actively. The current recruitment 'policy' is that God 'will bring' new members; so far this approach has brought five new members in the past twenty years. My initial overtures to the community and my eventual arrival were interpreted as a 'sign' from God.

I came across God's Way by accident; I had been writing to the leaders of a variety of religious and ethical communities in the USA, some 'closed', some open to 'outsiders', during the initial stages of my doctoral research. In these letters, I introduced myself as a student researcher interested in their community and belief systems. My research was 'overt' at this stage, but I included a note of ambiguity into my introduction by also presenting myself as a 'seeker' of alternative ways of living. Thus, I presented a dual identity; this was not a lie as such, as at that time I was interested in seeking out alternative ways of living. I received a number of replies and invitations to visit. However, I was most interested in my letter from Isaac the leader of God's Way community. In that initial letter he outlined their belief system and some of their history. We struck up a short correspondence during which I stressed an interest in visiting as a researcher, but also emphasised my 'seeker' role. Isaac then passed my correspondence on to his niece, Rachel, and she became my new correspondent from the community. We wrote to each other for the next six months during which it became clear that the group was interpreting my interest as a 'sign' from God and that I was a new member to be 'brought from overseas'. I went along with this deception, as it was clear from Isaac's initial letters that only potential members, as opposed to researchers, could visit the community. On arrival, following almost a year of correspondence, I assumed the role of 'new' member and later initiate to the community; one who had been sent by God, from overseas. I judged my successful 'role performance' through the fact that I was quickly accepted as a provisional member and assigned to the social category of 'adolescent', which included all community members (irrespective of age), who were not married with children. Marriage and children brought status and authority in the community, without them, you occupied a lowly place in the social hierarchy. This status suited me as it gave me greater licence to make mistakes without damaging my 'role performance'. I lived on the community for just under a year. I maintained contact with Rachel my key informant for several years following my fieldwork until our correspondence ended abruptly.

The community is a ranch, which is isolated from neighbouring farms through local topography, which is hilly. The heart of the community is the chapel and the communal dining room, where everyone eats together at every mealtime. A number of small houses circle the centre and these are home to the various family groupings. Single members are attached to a family group, thus I was housed with Isaac's family. The internal design of all the buildings is open plan, with no doors in the door frames. Curtains can be drawn in door frames to maintain privacy when using the bathroom or sleeping. All bedrooms are shared and curtains are never drawn unless the room is in use at night. This design works to maximise a communal ethos and minimise feelings of individuality and privacy. It also allows community members to monitor each other and thus enforce norms of behaviour and belief. The only time one is truly alone is in the bathroom and even then, the noise from conversations can be heard coming from surrounding rooms. The only 'quiet' space was the chapel, but this was rarely used for private study or worship and for members to have sat alone in the chapel would have generated disapproval. The ranch has several acres of land for growing crops and they keep chickens and horses.

The community view themselves as God's 'chosen' people and that only they will survive the end of the world, which they believe to be quickly approaching. Their belief system, which will be explored in later chapters, is steeped in American Protestantism and is fundamentalist in orientation. God's Way will be used as a central case study to explore the fundamentalist worldview. However, other examples will also be used to demonstrate the diversity of Protestant fundamentalism, its commonalities and differences.

The Structure of the Book

To understand the appeal of religious fundamentalism in even the most modern of societies it is important to explore a number of related questions:

- What is religious fundamentalism?
- What is the specific nature of American Protestant fundamentalism?
- What are the characteristics of a fundamentalist worldview?
- What is the appeal of this particular set of beliefs and worldview?
- Why does religious fundamentalism emerge and thrive in modern and late modern societies?

This book aims to answer these questions and explore these themes. The book's central contention is that to fully understand this phenomenon, one must get to its heart, which is its worldview. One cannot understand fundamentalist beliefs or actions in the world without appreciating their source of agency, which lies in their worldview.

This book is structured in such a way that it will take the reader through the different key characteristics of the Protestant fundamentalist worldview. Chapters 2 and 3 set the scene for the subsequent chapters by further contextualising Protestant fundamentalism, historically and theoretically. Chapter 2 reviews the issue of definitions: what is a fundamentalist and are all fundamentalisms (regardless of their specific religious provenance) the same? Is a unitary definition possible and desirable? The long running academic debate on this topic will be discussed. The contrasts and connections between Christian fundamentalists and other Christian groupings, such as evangelicals, charismatics and conservatives, that are often mistakenly labelled as 'fundamentalist' will be examined. Building on this discussion of definitions and characteristics the chapter will end by outlining the five key characteristics of the typical fundamentalist worldview: chosen-ness; orthodoxy and orthopraxy; separation and opposition; apocalypticism; and (re)action in the world. The following chapters will focus on one of these characteristics, which will run as a theme in that chapter. Thus readers will literally be taken through a fundamentalist worldview and see how its different elements work together to inform action.

Chapter 3 discusses the historical roots of American Protestant fundamentalism and the socio-political forces that caused its emergence and growth. When and why did this variety of fundamentalism emerge in the world's most 'modern' nation? American-style Protestant fundamentalism is uniquely related to the socio-political structure of the USA, which needs to be contextualised, for example, in foundation views of national destiny and 'chosen nation' status; in an identification of White Protestants as 'true' Americans; and in the constitutional separation of state and religion. There will be an outline of the emergence of Protestant fundamentalism in the USA, with its roots in the modernisation of the late nineteenth century, where factors such as mass immigration, Biblical Criticism, urbanisation and industrialisation prompted the emergence of groups, who sought to critique modernity and stress the 'fundamentals' of faith. The politicisation of what were initially theological issues and the failure of early political campaigns will be discussed. The chapter will end by exploring the growth of fundamentalist communities in the post-war era and the increasingly influential political action of these groups will be examined.

Chapters 4–8 all focus on a different aspect of worldview. Chapter 4 primarily focuses on the core belief in being 'chosen' and how this is the foundation of the entire fundamentalist worldview. A sense of being 'chosen' is both a shared communal identity and a personal identity. However, claims of being 'chosen' or communal uniqueness are not uncommon through history or across different religions – so how do such groups maintain this view of their own uniqueness and how does it withstand competing claims to special status? Chapter 5 focuses on how fundamentalists live out their sense of being 'chosen' through their everyday lives, where orthodoxy and orthopraxy are paramount. If one is 'chosen' then all activities become sites for expression of religious devotion and commitment. Therefore, behaviour is strictly monitored and controlled, especially around morality, gender and sexuality. The role of commitment mechanisms (rituals, beliefs, activities) that are used to reinforce and maintain faith over time will be discussed, particularly the use of Biblical literalism. Chapter 6 explores the apocalypticism that is part of the fundamentalist worldview. Fundamentalists are profoundly apocalyptic and a belief in the end of the world adds agency and urgency to their beliefs and activities. Apocalypticism is an important form of reinforcement for their belief in being 'chosen'. This chapter will also look at the importance of 'signs'. It will also look at what happens when the end of the world does not happen as predicted. Chapter 7 discusses fundamentalists' relationship with the 'outside' world; fundamentalists have a strong oppositional worldview which reinforces their sense of being 'chosen' and creates real and symbolic 'enemies' to fight back against. The nature of this oppositional worldview and its impact on activities and beliefs will be explored; especially around political action. The exploration of worldview ends in Chapter 8 with a discussion of fundamentalist political action and radicalism. What impact have they had and what impact might they have? Their preoccupation with education, moral and family issues is discussed. Differing political positions will be reviewed particularly in relation to the extent to which such groups wish to change the secular world and to what extent they wish to abandon it.

Chapter 9, the final chapter, places American Protestant fundamentalism (and its worldview) back into the broader spectrum of global fundamentalism. It returns to some of the issues explored in Chapter 2 around definitions, such as, are fundamentalists more alike than different. It explores the reasons behind the global growth in religious fundamentalism. It will discuss some of the consequences of this growth and whether it poses a serious socio-political threat in the world or whether it is transitionary phase.

Chapter 2

'Same or Different'? Defining Fundamentalism?

American exceptionalism in relation to participation in religion, as measured by church membership and attendance, as well as beliefs held is well documented (see for example, Martin, 2005, Davie, 2002, Berger, 1999). After Eire, the USA maintains the highest church-going population of all western nations, with 42 per cent of the American population attending a weekly church service (Gallup, 2008). This figure has remained consistent since Gallup pollsters started surveys of religious attendance in the 1930s (Gallup, 2009). The previous chapter discussed the dominance of the Secularisation Thesis (Bruce, 2002), and American exceptionalism has always proved a theoretical challenge to the view that as societies modernise they will secularise and attendance will drop. This phenomenon has been charted across Western Europe (Wilson, 1966, Bruce, 2001, Bruce, 2002) but although the USA is a secular state, in that there is no state church and a constitutional separation between religion and the state; it does not follow this pattern with regard to participation in formal, institutionalised forms of religion. American exceptionalism is one of the factors that has led to the Secularisation Thesis being modified to apply only to the western European context (Martin, 2005, Davie, 2002, Berger, 1999).

Religious surveys and polls in the USA also appear to show high levels of fundamentalist beliefs (Ammerman, 1991 and 1993, Plutzer and Berkman, 2008) and by implication a large population of fundamentalist Christians, specifically Protestants. This has led to the populist view (which plays on Anti-American stereotypes common in Europe) that the USA is home to the world's biggest population of religious fundamentalists; an assertion that never fails to surprise, given the fact that the USA remains the most advanced, most 'modern' of modern societies. However, it is an assertion that needs to be tempered with two facts; firstly, polls do not directly ask people if they are 'fundamentalists' (and if they did few would self-identify with that label, as will be discussed later in this chapter). Secondly, this view is based on people appearing to believe a series of core beliefs that are commonly associated with 'fundamentalism'.

For example, successive Gallup polls in the 1980s and 1990s (see for example, Gallup and O'Connell, 1986, Gallup and Castelli, 1989, Ammerman, 1993, Plutzer and Berkman, 2008) showed that 40 per cent of Americans believed that the Bible was the 'actual word' of God and that 44 per cent supported Creationism. Gallup found that 19 per cent of the population could be categorised as 'evangelical' based on adherence to Biblical literalism, Creationism and claims to having been 'born again'. The Gallup polls were specifically looking at evangelicals, as opposed to fundamentalists, but if we assume (Ammerman, 1993, 6) those fundamentalists are subsumed within this group then a significant population must exist. More recently, a CNN/Time poll in 2002 (Plutzer and Berkman, 2008) found a similarly high level of Biblical literalism among Americans. The same poll also found that 44 per cent of Americans agree that Creationism is the best explanation for humanity's beginnings and that 59 per cent believe that there is a coming apocalypse as foretold in the Bible. Apocalypticism is another belief common among evangelicals and fundamentalists.

These poll results demonstrate that the core beliefs of evangelical and fundamentalist Christianity are widely held in the USA. However, it needs to be noted that answering a pollster's questions does not necessarily imply action on the part of the individual; it may just demonstrate sympathy with that belief position. It is also a well-known methodological fact that individuals have a tendency to lie in surveys and of course, how they answer also depends greatly on how the questions themselves are worded. Thus, the actual numbers of 'active' evangelicals and fundamentalists in the USA will be lower than surveys suggest, but their significance remains undiminished (Plutzer and Berkman, 2008). The tendency to lump American evangelical and fundamentalist Christians together in surveys on conservative Christianity not only leads to over-estimations of fundamentalist populations but also more importantly ignores key differences between these two forms of Protestant Christianity (Barr, 1977, Marsden 1980, 1984). Therefore, it is important that we explore definitional issues, to ascertain who is and is not a 'fundamentalist'. To do this it is important to start with the word's origins and review the original meaning of the term 'fundamentalist'.

Origins of the Word

The history of American Protestant fundamentalism will be discussed in greater detail in the next chapter; but by the early twentieth century conservative Protestants had started to form coalitions to challenge the theological trends in Biblical criticism (and revisionism) and Liberal theology that had emerged in the nineteenth century (Marsden, 1980). Liberal theology had been a theological response to modernism, secularism and evolutionary theory. For example, Liberal theology viewed Biblical scripture as allegorical or symbolic rather than literal. The Bible was acknowledged as a man-made text, rather than the 'word' of God. These conservative Protestant groups were predominantly interested in theological matters rather than effecting socio-political changes, although as will be argued in the next chapter; their emergence was precipitated by wider socio-economic changes. Within this context, the term 'fundamentalist' was coined. It was first used in a series of twelve pamphlets, called *The Fundamentals: A Testimony of Truth*, which were edited by A.C. Dixon; they were published in the United States between 1910 and 1915 (Dollar, 1973). The pamphlets (Dollar, 1973, Marsden,

1980, Ammerman, 1991) reiterated a return to the so-called 'fundamentals of faith' and a rejection of those organisations and beliefs that sought to undermine it. This return to 'the fundamentals' asserted a view that the Bible was the inerrant word of God; that believers should lead morally upright lives informed directly by scripture; that 'true' believers should live separate lives from non-believers, else they may be morally and spiritually 'corrupted'; and that scientific theories, like evolution, should be rejected. It also called for believers to challenge the spread of secularism (and liberalism) within key social institutions, such as schools. People who agreed with these principles began to call themselves 'fundamentalists', although even then many preferred to use alternative terms, such as, 'true' believers.

By 1920, the term 'fundamentalist' was commonly used (Barr, 1977) to refer to those who sought to fight back against and reject modernist influences on scripture, for example, those who presented such biblical teachings as the Virgin Birth to be allegory rather than 'truth'. At this time the label 'fundamentalist' incorporated a diverse range of Protestant groups, from 'extreme' hard-line fundamentalists to those who might identify themselves as 'traditionalists', 'conservatives', or 'evangelicals'. The label was theological rather than political, identifying a theological desire to go back to and reiterate 'the basics' (Barr, 1977). By the 1940s the label, 'fundamentalist', became increasingly difficult to sustain, and divisions started to emerge between conservatives, evangelicals, and those who preferred to self-identify as 'fundamentalists'. The reasons behind these divisions will be explored in Chapter 3, but suffice to say that by the 1940s a specific 'fundamentalist' identity had emerged that saw itself as separate from other forms of conservative Protestantism, particularly Evangelicalism (Marsden, 1980, 1984). In the post-war era 'fundamentalist' Protestants became increasingly politicised, seeking to act in the world, and adopt a hard-line, no compromise stance. Thus, the word 'fundamentalist' (and correspondingly 'fundamentalism') was originally associated with American Protestantism and was initially a theological term (Barr, 1977).

'Fundamentalism' in Popular Usage

The word 'fundamentalism' entered populist usage in 1979, following the Iranian Revolution. Before then the word had tended to be only used in relation to American Protestantism. However, western journalists struggled to describe the new Iranian state's brand of Islam to a western 'audience' with little awareness or knowledge of Islam generally. The new regime's stress on literalism (of the Koran in this case); the belief that their interpretation of Islam was the 'true' way; their strict emphasis on moral issues; their 'back to basics' version of Islam and hard-line approach to anything that deviated from this version, soon led commentators to see parallels with Protestant fundamentalism. Hence, a word that had previously only been a theological term used to describe a particular brand of American Protestantism was used to categorise a particular version of Islam in the Middle East, far removed from the word's etymological or historical roots (Gupta, 1993, Munson, 1995, Scott Jones, 2009). The word soon became widely used to describe all varieties of religious extremism and radicalism. It quickly lost its original theological meaning and became a sociological and political label. Since then the word has become increasingly overused and misused.

A Pejorative Label?

'Fundamentalism' and 'fundamentalist' are two of the most misused, and misunderstood, terms in current everyday usage. 'Fundamentalist' is often used synonymously with 'terrorist', particularly in relation to Islamic terrorism. Similarly, 'fundamentalist' has been used interchangeably with such terms as 'conservative', 'traditionalist', and 'orthodox'. Such semantic misunderstandings can lead to the lumping together of all sorts of disparate religious and non-religious groups (Gupta, 1993, Munson, 1995).

'Fundamentalists' are not necessarily proponents of terror tactics. Terrorist groups seek to advance political protest and change by using, or at least threatening to use, violence or terror. Such groups are motivated by a variety of different agendas that do not necessarily involve religion, including fighting for specific political ideologies, ethnic or nationalist concerns, or against an authoritarian state. The designation 'terrorist' is controversial as it is typically applied by those who believe themselves to be terrorised, whereas those involved in such acts may see themselves in a more favourable light, for example, as 'freedom fighters'. Religious concerns can be a motivation for many terrorist groups, particularly where ethnic identity and religion combine, as it did, for example, in Northern Ireland; but typically 'terrorist groups' use religious identity in a symbolic way to rally people to their cause: religion is not their raison d'être. However, most religious fundamentalists are not terrorists, and many would see the taking of life as 'evil' as they view all life as 'sacred' and 'God given'. Yet others do utilise terrorist tactics to achieve their political aims, for example, the attacking of abortion clinics by some Protestant fundamentalists in the United States.

'Fundamentalist' has become an increasingly pejorative term that has been used to label all forms of religico-political groups, but Islamic ones in particular. In the post-9/11 world, there has been a rise in Islamophobia and a growing intolerance in many communities towards racial and religious diversity (Kaplan, 2006). Stereotypes facilitate the demonisation of communities and create an environment for 'moral panics' that portray all Muslims as 'fundamentalists' and by implication potential terrorists. The easy interchange of the words 'terrorist', 'fundamentalist' and 'Islam' can be seen in a review of newspaper reporting over the past decade and a half (Runnymede Trust, 1997). Typically, 'fundamentalist' has become in common parlance at least, a term of abuse and a useful shorthand for describing an individual or group as 'extremist', 'hard-line', dogmatic' and 'traditional'. The increasingly pejorative use of the word has led many to reject its use altogether, even within social science research (see for example, Gupta, 1993 and Munson, 1995). However, censoring language is rarely a useful strategy for challenging racism, religious discrimination or 'extremism'. Rather it is vital that we use the term correctly and with precision, in other words when we label an individual or community as 'fundamentalist' we need to ensure we understand exactly what that means and how they differ from other types of religious or political communities.

Who Is and Is Not a Fundamentalist

The common grouping together of evangelicals and fundamentalists was discussed briefly at the start of this chapter and is an all too common occurrence. Similarly, other forms of conservative Christianity can often also be misunderstood as 'evangelical' or 'fundamentalist', because they may share some common beliefs. The conservative shift that has been a key global trend of religion in the past forty years, particularly in relation to Christianity and Islam, can lead to a stereotype that all conservatives are alike (Scott Jones, 2009). The conservative shift within Christianity, for example, is a continuum with more moderate conservatives, such as traditionalists, at one end and the more dogmatic, 'hard-line' stance of fundamentalists at the other. Groups that may all belong to the conservative shift may not associate themselves as being like other members of that broad category and in fact may view them with as much contempt as they might a liberal church.

All religions have a conservative or orthodox wing, as well as a liberal wing; there may be overlaps in beliefs and practices, but being 'conservative' or 'orthodox' are not the same as being 'fundamentalist.' Orthodox Jews, for example, may stress what might be called the 'fundamentals' of their faith, but they do so for theological reasons; there is no sense of the political agency attached to beliefs that one would expect to see with fundamentalist Jews. Similarly, being a 'traditionalist' in one's religious beliefs and practices, whereby one might reject modern hymns in church or new versions of the Bible, certainly does not mean that one is a 'fundamentalist'. In a similar vein, devotion and commitment to one's religious beliefs and practices is also not synonymous with being a 'fundamentalist'; indeed, the view that devotion equates with fundamentalism is a common mistake that particularly leads to the racist stereotyping of Muslim communities that can be seen today in many Western nations.

Evangelicals are most commonly misrepresented as 'fundamentalists'. One reason for this is that both have a shared theological root in the late nineteenth century and both shared a common goal to challenge modernism. This shared history will be explored in more detail in Chapter 3. Evangelical Protestants share many beliefs with fundamentalist Protestants, including:

- An adherence to Biblical literalism and inerrancy
- A belief in Creationism as the only viable account for man's existence
- A belief in a coming apocalypse as foretold and outlined in the Bible

- A belief that only the 'saved' will survive this apocalypse
- They hold traditional views on the family and gender
- A sense of patriotism that equates White Protestantism with being a 'true' American
- They challenge the separation of private/public in contemporary society
- They place a strong emphasis on traditional, Biblically directed morality
- A belief that God has 'called' or 'chosen' them

However there are a number of key differences; differences that ultimately caused American evangelicals and fundamentalist to break from each other in the 1940s. Evangelicals hold the view that everyone has the potential to be 'saved' and become 'born again' (Barr, 1977, Marsden, 1984). Fundamentalists tend to have a more exclusive view of their relationship to God; they are specifically 'chosen' by God and those who are not 'chosen' are 'fallen'. The 'fallen' have no potential to become 'chosen'. Evangelicals actively proselytise to spread their religious message and thus potentially 'save' others. Fundamentalists see no point in preaching to the unconverted as they do not view them as 'redeemable' (Scott, 1996). Evangelicals' view of being 'born again' is something which they acknowledge can be experienced by members of other Protestant denominations; they do not make claims to an exclusive relationship with God, whereas fundamentalists believe that only they are 'chosen' and thus view their relationship to God as unique (Barr, 1977). Fundamentalists would disparage other denominations or religions' identification as 'chosen'. Evangelicals' more open attitude to their relationship with God and their view of other communities, means that they are more willing to work with other denominations to achieve shared religious, political or communal goals. They will participate in interdenominational networks (Dollar, 1973, Ammerman, 1991). Fundamentalists' stress on exclusivity means that they find working within interdenominational networks challenging; as they find it hard to compromise. Finally, evangelicals have a more relaxed and open attitude to modern, secular society; they are willing to accommodate it and work within its structures and institutions to effect change (Barr, 1977, Dollar, 1973). Fundamentalists reject this position and work against modern, secular, society with the ultimate aim to change it, to reflect their way of life. These are obviously broad characteristics; communities and churches will differ within these generic categories of 'evangelical' and 'fundamentalist'. All groups need to be placed and understood within their own social context. Fundamentalists are people whose desire to reiterate a particular version of the 'basics' of their beliefs intertwines with a political agency to act in the secular world (Marty and Appleby, 1991).

Same or Different?

The problems with using the word 'fundamentalist' have already been discussed in relation to its misuse as a term of abuse. However, another issue that surrounds the use of the word focuses on its utility when used to describe groups who are not American Protestants. Can we really label groups, across different religions, with diverse histories and cultural contexts, as the same? Many theorists, such as Munson (1995) argue that we cannot apply to different religious movements a word ('fundamentalist') that was used originally to refer to specific theological concerns within American Protestantism. Can we really compare the Taliban with the Gush Emunim or the Westboro Baptist church? Moreover, should we? Similarly, as Gupta (1993) notes, in lumping different groups together under a common label, do we end up overemphasising commonalities over important religious and cultural differences? These are legitimate concerns and many theorists prefer to focus on contextualising rather than categorising (Gupta, 1993). However, would such an approach miss important theoretical or theological angles due to a reticence to compare similar groups? After all within the sociology of religion we show no great theoretical discomfort with comparing disparate groups within other categories, such as 'cult', 'New Age' or indeed 'religion'. These categories have been widely debated and contested but they are still used because they serve a semantic and analytical purpose; they facilitate understanding of a phenomenon or community in a broader sense. Using a label or category does not necessarily imply that one cannot also emphasise the importance of context. Others have called for an outright rejection of the word within the social sciences (Elias, 1999). Rejecting the use of words that are already part of the common language seems pointless as colloquial understandings will remain.

Marty and Appleby (1991) and Bruce (2008) make the same important point that academics love participating in semantic debates; indeed the sociology of religion alone is riddled with such examples. Such debates soon become akin to Mediaeval musings about angels and pinheads; possibly interesting but not that helpful in a methodological or theoretical sense. The 'crustaceans' debate[1] generated by Marty and Appleby's (1991) 'family resemblances' model of fundamentalism is a prime example of this in action. We can become so preoccupied with words that we overlook their base utility; words like 'fundamentalist' or 'religion' already exist, are commonly used, and are generally understood. There is little sense, if you will, in reinventing words and 'something' has to be called *something*. Marty and Appleby (1991) take the view that 'fundamentalist' is a useful label and that different groups can be assigned this label. They make the point that differences and context are important and should not be overlooked, but then neither should an appreciation of similarities. After all, if we cannot identify commonalities how can we confront and engage with fundamentalists in the real world?

---

1   See *Contention* 4 (Spring) 1995, for the articles relating to this debate.

The 'Family Resemblances' Model

Marty and Appleby (1991) argue that the labels 'fundamentalist'/'fundamentalism' are meaningful and useful. They stress the commonalities across 'fundamentalisms' and identify five key characteristics common to all varieties of fundamentalism. They argue that fundamentalists share enough common features or 'resemblances'; they use the analogy of cousins. Cousins share a common relative and although are not identical, typically share some physical features that can identify their common kinship; perhaps, for example, they all have their grandfather's nose. Marty and Appleby (1991) argue that fundamentalists are like cousins, we can identify common features that show a sense of 'kinship' but we can also appreciate key differences. This approach to defining fundamentalism is known as the 'family resemblances' model. It is a model that does not negate historical or cultural contextualisation, rather it emphasises the need to locate commonalities as much as 'differences'. The five volumes of the 'Fundamentalism Project' (1991, 1993a, 1993b, 1994, 1995) vividly demonstrate the importance of context for understanding what Marty and Appleby label 'fundamentalisms'; they also provide a good example of the utility of cross-cultural comparison of 'fundamentalisms'. The 'family resemblances' approach to defining fundamentalism has become widely adopted and is the approach used in this book.

Marty and Appleby (1991), among others, have argued that fundamentalists are different from those that could be categorised as 'traditional' or 'orthodox' because they seek to engage directly with the modern world and change it: in other words fundamentalists, and therefore fundamentalism, is radical and political in that it has an agenda for socio-political as well as religious change. Marty and Appleby (1991) acknowledge that religious fundamentalism is all about acting in the world. Fundamentalists anticipate the end of the world but they are not passively awaiting the apocalypse in some isolated retreat. They know what they want, believe that they have a higher purpose to serve, and believe that through the guidance of God they will ultimately get what they desire. The 'family resemblances' model has five key characteristics and they focus on the agency and activity of fundamentalists. Marty and Appleby's (1991, ix–x) five key 'family resemblances' are as follows:

1. *A sense of fighting back*: Fundamentalists are not retreatist, they see it as their role to 'fight back' against the socio-political forces associated with secular modernity; that they perceive to be threatening their way of life. As they believe themselves to be God's 'chosen', they consider themselves the only ones who can do this job 'right'. Often they see this 'fight' as one that has to be won for spiritual, social, and national reasons. The willingness to 'fight back' and stand up for what they believe in lends power to their sense of self-worth and agency to act. For example, American Protestant fundamentalists view themselves as fighting for 'America's soul'.

2. *A sense of fighting against*: Although they are 'fighting back' against secular modernity in general, fundamentalists have specific targets for their

political action. Their oppositional worldview facilitates the identification of 'enemies' and 'enemy targets'. 'Fighting against' usually involves the construction of extensive demonologies of selected 'enemies', which utilise stereotype, racism, homophobia, caricature, and so forth, to demonise opponents and specific targets. An example of this would be Iran's depiction of the USA as 'the Great Satan'. Chapter 7 discusses demonisation in greater detail. The identification and targeting of specific individuals, groups, social institutions and so forth, allows fundamentalists to focus their considerable political energies; it also offers a simplistic and easily communicated explanation for socio-political problems, that followers of any background can absorb. For example, the targeting of western 'brands', like Coca Cola and McDonalds, by Islamic fundamentalists in Malaysia. The brand becomes synonymous with westernisation, modernisation, secularism and all that is perceived to be wrong with Malaysia. Thus, complex socio-economic issues become simplified and easily digested via the anger towards the 'brand'. This 'brand' targeting becomes real through actual attacks on McDonalds or KFC restaurants. Another example would be the attacks, by Islamic fundamentalists, on western tourists in Egypt; tourists become an easily identified symbol for the social and economic inequalities that drive Islamic fundamentalism in Egypt.

3. *A sense of fighting for*: Fundamentalists have particular social, economic, or political goals that they 'fight for'. This allows communal energies to be channelled and used efficiently; it also allows individuals to remain focused and goal-oriented. Protestant fundamentalists in the USA tend to 'fight for' socio-moral issues, such as the overturning of abortion legislation, the fight against gay rights, and the restricting of sex education in schools. Chapter 8 discusses such campaigns further. In the Middle East, Islamic fundamentalists 'fight for' socio-political issues, such as restricting foreign influence, regime change, the establishment of an Islamic state, or the assertion of national, ethnic or religious identities.

4. *A sense of fighting with*: Fundamentalists are communalistic in nature and therefore have a community to 'fight with'. This community is viewed as a community of 'true believers'; a belief that gives them a strong shared identity. A sense of community is also created through the oppositionality, orthodoxy, and orthopraxy that characterises their worldview. These communities are established in opposition to the 'outside' world and this sense of separation and opposition reinforces their sense of group identity and difference. Living a strictly religious life with set codes of conduct further creates a sense of communal identity and cohesion in an instrumental and symbolic sense. How they choose to conduct their lives further facilitates their sense of separation from the 'outside' and compounds their sense of specialness. Fundamentalist communities can use their size and networking skills to pool resources, raise funds, and rally members. The fund raising abilities of Protestant fundamentalists in the USA, is a good example of

this and successive Republican presidential campaigns have benefited in the past thirty years. The ability to generate large campaign 'war chests' gives fundamentalists a degree of political power and influence; at the very least political lip service is paid to their concerns. In Egypt, Islamic fundamentalists use their networks to establish communal resources, for example, free healthcare and education, which can boost communal morale and be a lure for new recruits.

5. *A sense of fighting under God*: Fundamentalists do all the other forms of 'fighting' for one reason: they are 'chosen' by God. In other words, they consider God to be on their side and that they are doing God's bidding. This belief gives tremendous agency and power to fundamentalist action and generates high levels of self-belief; with God on your side how can you lose. Thus, fundamentalists view their political actions as not mere politicking but part of a greater divine plan; this makes fundamentalists formidable opponents. In addition their belief that this is God's 'work' makes them uncompromising in the face of opposition, but also succeeds in making it difficult for fundamentalists to work within wider political networks as they refuse to 'make deals' and seek compromises to enact change.

These five 'family resemblances' are socio-political characteristics; religious fundamentalism also operates within a set of theological characteristics, which draw on the religious tradition to which they belong. It is important to appreciate theological differences across fundamentalisms, although again, there will be commonalities.

Theological Characteristics of American Protestant Fundamentalism

American Protestant fundamentalists share the following key beliefs (Barr 1977, Ammerman, 1987):

1. *A belief in the inerrancy of the Bible*, specifically the King James version. They take the Bible as the actual, literal, word of God, unedited and not revised.
2. *A belief in the imminent Second Coming of Christ* as foretold in the Bible. The return of Christ is viewed as part of a global apocalypse that will involve a final battle between the forces of good and evil, in which the 'chosen' will prevail and be 'saved' and the 'fallen' will perish.
3. *A belief that they have been 'chosen'* as individuals and communities by God to do his work. Being 'chosen' is not something that can be conferred on an individual by simply following a proscribed set of religious rules; rather it is believed that God actively seeks out and 'chooses' the individual to be 'chosen'. The experience of being 'chosen' is individual and confers 'full' membership into the wider community of 'chosen'. Thus, it is a God-

given status and one that can be 'removed' if the individual in question does not maintain high standards of conduct and faith.

4. *Moral absolutism*, based on strict adherence to Biblically derived morality. Absolutism implies a Manichaean view of moral issues, i.e. something is either morally 'right' or 'wrong', there is no sense of moral ambiguity. For example, to a moral absolutist, abortion is quite simply morally 'wrong', irrespective of circumstances or medical arguments.

5. *A stress on Orthodoxy*. They view themselves as the only 'true' believers, believing in the 'right' way. The Bible serves as a template for how they view their beliefs. Orthodoxy can be seen in their view that what they believe and how they express their beliefs is the only 'true' version of Christianity.

6. *A stress on Orthopraxy*. They view themselves as the only 'believers' who live their lives the 'right' way. The Bible serves as a guide for how they conduct their lives. Orthopraxy is demonstrated through dress codes, special diets, marriage rules, views on gender and so forth.

7. *A dualist, oppositional view of the world*. Protestant fundamentalists view the world as divided between 'true' believers and everyone else who might be labelled as the 'fallen', which creates an inevitable sense of oppositionality.

These theological characteristics are specific to Protestant fundamentalists. For obvious reasons Islamic, Jewish, or other varies of fundamentalism would not share the second characteristic listed above. They would however feature versions of the other six characteristics, in addition to ones specific to their own religious context. All fundamentalists are literalists who take scripture as inerrant; for Islamic fundamentalists this would be the Koran and for Jewish fundamentalists the Torah and Talmud. Other forms of fundamentalism, such as Buddhist or Hindu, will show lower levels of literalism, as these traditions place less importance on the belief, in one 'true' scripture. Protestant fundamentalists focus on an apocalypse featuring Christ's return; again, this is unique to Christian varieties of fundamentalism. However, Islamic fundamentalism also shows high levels of apocalypticism, particularly in the post 9/11 context. As will be discussed in Chapter 6, monotheistic faiths have a greater tendency to exhibit apocalyptic beliefs, so other varieties of religious fundamentalism may not show this theological feature. All forms of religious fundamentalism feature characteristics four to seven listed above, albeit within their specific traditions. For example, Jewish or Islamic fundamentalists will draw on their specific sacred scriptures to derive their moral codes, and a sense of orthodoxy and orthopraxy.

The seven theological characteristics of Protestant fundamentalism will be discussed in more detail in later chapters that explore aspects of this worldview. These theological characteristics can also be found among religious conservatives and some traditionalists, but what defines fundamentalists is the extreme and absolute degree to which they adhere to and apply these characteristics.

Outlining a Worldview

Drawing on Marty and Appleby's 'family resemblances' model (1991), which gives a socio-political definition of religious fundamentalism, alongside the seven theological characteristics discussed above, we can outline a worldview from which to explore religious fundamentalism in general and American Protestant fundamentalism in particular. This worldview features the following elements:

- *A belief in having been 'chosen'.* The central component of this worldview is that individuals and communities are uniquely 'chosen' by God to do his work. There is a view that they are the 'chosen' people. This belief therefore implies that there are also individuals and communities who are not 'chosen' and these are usually categorised by terms like the 'fallen'.
- *A commitment to Orthodoxy and orthopraxy.* Living a religious life in the way that fundamentalists perceive God wants, is the key to reinforcing and maintaining their belief system. A sense of being 'chosen' creates great pressure to live and believe in the 'right' way. Scripture becomes a tool to organise how to live and how to believe.
- *Apocalypticism.* A belief in an imminent, pre-ordained, end of the world infuses this worldview with a sense of urgency; the cosmic clock is literally ticking. Apocalyptic belief also places action in a broader context and gives it meaning beyond instrumental or immediate everyday goals. Apocalyptic rhetoric is also useful for rallying individuals and communities as Chapter 6 will discuss.
- *Oppositionality and separatism.* A belief in being 'chosen' establishes an oppositional view of the world into 'chosen' and 'fallen'. This inevitably creates a sense of separatism and fundamentalists often use language like 'contamination' or 'pollution' to refer to the secular world and non-fundamentalist communities. Such a view of the 'outside' world facilitates the creation of political targets and 'enemies'; as well as creating physical and symbolic boundaries that help reinforce fundamentalist communal identities.
- *Political action in the world.* Fundamentalists are radical in the sense of having an agenda for socio-political action. They seek to challenge, critique and change the secular, modern world in which they live. Plans for political action are usually linked to a future time when their 'chosen' status will allow them to literally inherit the world. Political activity is seen as God's 'work' and is therefore seen as 'right'. Political activities can vary from single-issue campaigns to revolutionary efforts to destabilise governments. Apocalyptic beliefs present political action as contributing to a bigger divine plan beyond the immediate issue or campaign.

These five aspects of worldview have been discussed separately but they should be viewed as interlinked; each working off and with the other elements. Diagrammatically the worldview might look like this:

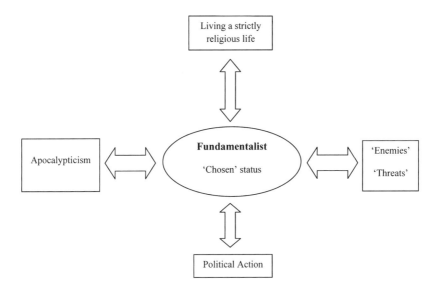

The sense of being 'chosen' is the base on which the rest of the worldview is built, without this belief the other elements would cease to be as important or more importantly make sense; why worry about the end of the world or of taking political action against so-called 'enemies', if you did not consider yourself to be 'chosen'. The other elements work off and then reinforce this sense of being 'chosen'. Fundamentalists live a strictly religious life because they consider themselves God's 'chosen' people; in the living of their lives in this way, they in turn reinforce their identity as the 'chosen', setting themselves apart from others, who are by default not 'chosen', as they do not conduct their lives in this way. Living a strictly moral life, with set rules and behaviours based on interpretations of sacred scripture, also allows the everyday 'doing' of this worldview; everyday life demonstrates religious beliefs and commitments, while also making them real and meaningful for followers (Ammerman, 1993).

A belief in the end of the world, similarly, is made sense of through this view of being 'chosen'; when the world ends the 'chosen' will survive in some form of 'heaven on earth' while their enemies, the 'non-believers' will perish. Apocalypticism validates their identity, political action, and way of life (Scott, 1996). Without this sense of a divine destiny, the view that they are 'chosen' would become problematic, lacking validation. In a similar vein how they view themselves, as 'chosen' creates potential, real or symbolic, 'enemies' or 'threats' to their communities and beliefs. It does this as it creates an opposition between 'chosen' and 'fallen'. Again, if there were no sense of opposition or 'enemies' the sense of being 'chosen' would lack validation; this is a version of 'othering' (Arens, 1980, Said, 1978) in that the 'fallen' are 'other' to the 'chosen', each identity constructed in relation (and opposition) to the other. Finally, the desire to act in the world and effect change is driven by this concept of being 'chosen'; one acts because one has been tasked with 'God's' work. Feeding into this is, of course, a sense of apocalyptic urgency; this work has to be done *now* and fits into a greater divine master plan. The construction of 'enemies', who exist in opposition to fundamentalists, creates a need for action and validates and gives significance to these actions. Thus, this is a worldview that is predicated on the belief in being 'chosen' and the other elements work to reinforce and validate this belief. However, this is a dynamic model; all the elements are important for the worldview to be sustained.

Marty and Appleby's (1991, ix–x) five 'family resemblances' are useful as they offer a framework for exploring the reasons why fundamentalism emerges (a point which will be explored in greater detail in subsequent chapters); and they also illustrate the socio-political attitude that fundamentalists adopt in their engagement with the world. This socio-political attitude is established by the fundamentalist worldview that has been outlined above. In Chapter 1, the role that worldviews play in explaining, interpreting, and establishing what 'reality' is (and is not) was discussed. Worldviews therefore, by implication, shape and direct our actions in 'reality' (Berger and Luckmann, 1966). How we see the world ('reality') directs our actions in it; at the same time, our actions in the world, and more importantly our interpretation of their consequences, impact back on to our worldview. This operates as a meaning feedback system; our actions might reinforce or validate our worldview, or cause it to be altered, dismantled or problematised in some way (Berger and Luckmann, 1966).

To illustrate, if our worldview maintains that illness is caused by evil spirits; then we presume that such spirits exist in the world ('reality'). We would act in ways to prevent possession by these spirits, such as, carrying special charms, saying special prayers or avoiding certain places or people. If we avoided illness then our actions would validate our worldview. However, if we fell ill, despite our actions, we would experience a brief moment of 'meaning crisis' (Berger and Luckmann, 1966, Geertz, 1966, Weber, 1991) which would need to be resolved by amending our worldview to accommodate further knowledge about evil spirits, such as, this particular charm did not work but maybe this other one will. Or our wider meaning system on which our worldview is built might provide a suitable 'explanation' such as invoking the concept of 'sin'; you become ill because you did not follow the established moral code. The 'crisis' does not threaten to destabilise of overthrow the existing worldview; that would only likely happen if the entire community became sick and traditional methods did not 'work'. In that instance, the community of believers might begin to question the nature of 'reality' and seek a new 'version'. Therefore, worldview and action work in conjunction with each other. Worldview directs action and actions make sense only through an understanding of worldview (Berger and Luckmann, 1966, Geertz, 1966).

Much of this chapter has focused on unitary definitions of religious fundamentalism, although it did highlight the specific theological characteristics of American Protestant fundamentalism. Unitary definitions allow us to look at fundamentalism in a broad theoretical sense and identify commonalities. However, contextualisation is important if we are to understand the exact nature of specific 'versions' of fundamentalism; such as why they might target a particular social issue in their political campaigns or why they conduct their lives in a specific way. The theological characteristics of Protestant fundamentalists in the USA make them different from other forms of fundamentalism in this sense. These characteristics emerged through their specific historical development and are embedded within their American cultural context. Thus, to understand fully the American Protestant fundamentalist worldview we must place them in their historical context.

Chapter 3

'True Americans': The Origins of Protestant Fundamentalism

At first glance the USA, a secular, consumer-driven society would seem the least likely place to find religious fundamentalism of any kind and certainly not in any large numbers. However, as discussed in the preceding chapters, America proves the exception to many established 'rules' in relation to religion's place in the modern, secular world. This is ironic given that the USA has a constitutional separation of state and church; yet it still shows higher levels of church attendance than most other western, secular nations, many of whom have state churches (Gallup, 2008, 2009). To illustrate, the UK has one of the lowest levels of church attendance in Europe, despite the existence of a state church; the Church of England (Bruce, 2002). To account for this irony and more importantly to explain why Protestant fundamentalism emerged in the USA; it is necessary to explore the history of Christianity, particularly Protestantism, in America.

American Style Protestantism

American Protestantism differs greatly from the varieties of Protestantism found historically and more contemporarily in Western Europe (Noll, 1992). European Protestantism is typically institutional, formalised, and marked by denominationalism (Ahlstrom, 1975, Noll, 1992). It often has close ties to the state. Noll (1992) characterises American Protestantism as having two key features; it is highly non-conformist and shows a profound lack of denominationalism. Both features are a result of two related events. Firstly, during the Colonial period large numbers of non-conformist English Protestants immigrated to the eastern USA. The Colonial government, eager for settlers, encouraged this migration. The non-conformists sought to escape the religious persecution that they had experienced in England and wished to establish settlements where they would be able to practise freely their faith. Other non-conformists, from Germany and Scandinavia, soon followed these English Protestants. Although the established English churches had a presence in the colonies, the Puritan churches overshadowed them and wielded greater influence within the local population. These English churches went into sharp decline following the War of Independence as they were associated with the British and thus deemed 'un-American'. The second event to influence American Protestantism, which followed the War of Independence, was the enacting of the Constitution, which enshrined in law the right to freedom of religion and established the constitutional separation of church and state (Noll, 1992).

The new nation would not have a state church and would stress secularism in state institutions. This meant that no one 'version' of Protestantism dominated or had state ordained institutional power. The absence of a state church and the large population of non-conformists created an environment that saw a constantly changing, experimental and fluid variety of Protestantism. Noll (1992) notes that the history of American Protestantism is, in a sense, a chronicle of successive religious 'experiments' of varying success. In such an environment, beliefs were more important than formal membership or even formalised worship (Ruthven, 1989). Many varieties of American Protestantism, particularly the 'frontier' versions in the western states, were often highly idiosyncratic and exhibited 'borrowings' from other traditions; a form of Protestant bricolage. Thus, glossalia, healing, and other elements of charismatic or Pentecostal Protestantism might be mixed with traditional hymns and Bible readings. American Protestantism could be eclectic, revivalist, evangelical and charismatic (Noll, 1992). There was a lot of experimentation and blending of styles and practices, without the strict denominational boundaries one might expect to see. That said some versions of Protestantism remained strictly demarcated from the experimental, for example, Puritan versions (Ahlstrom, 1975).

A Protestant Empire?

The Pilgrim Fathers, sailing on the 'Mayflower', and landing at Plymouth Rock in 1620, served as a Protestant nation-founding myth that placed White Protestants at the very birth of the nation. In a sense, this event, that became increasingly mythologised, served to reinforce the view that White Protestants were the 'true' Americans, who were there from the start. Even after Independence, White Protestants dominated the new republic in terms of demographics, and more importantly political power. Ahlstrom (1975: I: 165) describes the USA, in its first century as an independent nation, as a 'Protestant empire'. The 1850 census validates this view, showing that 90 per cent of the population were Protestant and 90 per cent of the population had been born there. The American national polity's messianic view of itself as a 'chosen' nation (Ahlstrom 1975: I: 183, Bellah, 1967), formed part of this Protestant hegemony and White Protestants saw themselves as doubly 'chosen'; through both their religious and national identities. They viewed themselves as 'keepers' of this national destiny. Prior to the Civil War there were only small populations of White Americans who were not Protestants (Ahlstrom, 1975). However, this Protestant hegemony would soon be challenged due to the related socio-economic processes of modernisation and a demographic shift that would alter the cultural composition of the USA forever.

Modernity and the Religion Problem

The shift for western nations from pre-modernity into modernity was gradual and involved interconnecting economic, social and cultural catalysts and processes. Weber (1992) and Berger (1967) both identify the Protestant Reformation of the sixteenth century as the event that sowed the seeds for the growth of modernity; giving rise to individualism, rationalism, and secularism. Marxist (1990) analysis identifies the Industrial Revolution and the shift toward an industrial based Capitalist economy in the eighteenth century. Both catalysts certainly established patterns of thinking and altered the structure of society in ways that can be identified as 'modern'. The idea of 'modernity' as an explicit project or agenda to shape and change western society was a product of the Enlightenment of the late eighteenth and early nineteenth century. The Enlightenment was a philosophical movement of the eighteenth century, led by Scottish and French philosophers who saw progress, rationality, logic and science as the keys to society's future development. Enlightenment philosophers, along with early social scientists, identified the 'modern' not just as a new era, but also as an opportunity to 'perfect' society. The Enlightenment privileged rationality, empiricism, science, logic, the idea of objective 'truth', secularism, individuality, and objectivity. It therefore challenged superstition, tradition, custom, autocracy, and authoritarianism (Callinicos, 2007). The modern era emerged fully in the nineteenth century from these religious, economic and philosophical 'revolutions'.

Modernity poses a direct challenge to religion; religion is based on faith-based knowledge, stresses subjective experience, and draws heavily on tradition and custom. Religion, in modernity, increasingly appears as a pre-modern 'relic' and many Enlightenment philosophers, as well as many of the early social scientists, saw the eradication of religion as a necessity in a modern society in order to 'free' individuals and social groups from pre-modern ties that would hold progress back (Rabinow, 1984, Callinicos, 2007). The rise of science and empiricism posed a critique to religion through the use of evidence to challenge long-standing, religious beliefs. The best example of this is Darwin's theory of evolution, which posed the first serious challenge to the religious account of Creation and had empirical evidence to prove it. However, advances in geology and palaeontology also challenged Biblical accounts; evidence emerged that proved the Earth was much older than scripture suggested and of course, there is no mention of dinosaurs in the Bible. By the second half of the nineteenth century modernity's initial challenge to religion centred on scientific evidence that contradicted Biblical accounts.

In both Europe and the USA, theologians and church leaders sought to meet the challenges of scientific scrutiny, by adopting a more critical stance towards scripture; and secondly by refocusing the church's mission on to social issues. The first approach was called Biblical Criticism and it views scriptures, like the Bible, as human-made, constructed texts; open to criticism, revision and editing. Texts were no longer to be viewed as the literal, word of God. This approach stressed the symbolic and allegorical nature of scripture and criticised the literalist position

(Barr, 1977). Biblical Criticism became a mainstream theological position and continues to dominate mainstream Christianity.

The second response to modernist empiricism and science was the rise in Liberal theology. Liberal theology sought to accommodate the modern era by accepting scientific theories, like Darwinism, alongside wider social changes. Liberals tended to accept Biblical Criticism and positively encouraged ecumenism (Barr, 1977, Noll, 1992). This approach shifts away from a dogmatic view of belief towards a socially engaged position that views the modern church's mission as a 'social gospel'. Charity work, poor relief, engaging in issues of inequality and so forth become more important that strict doctrine or 'blind faith'. This has been a useful strategy for many mainstream Protestant churches in the modern era, both in Europe and the USA (Lindberg, 2005).

The origins of American Protestant fundamentalism lie in this era of theological compromise in the face of modernity's advancement. The first half of the nineteenth century saw the growth, in the USA, of revivalist, evangelicalism, which was deeply millennialist (Noll, 1992, Marsden, 1980). Waves of 'awakenings' swept the nation as communities got caught up in millennial anticipation, for example the Millerites in 1844. These communities believed in the idea of 'Rapture'; that they would literally be swept off their feet and up to Heaven as the 'end of days' began and Jesus returned to Earth (Sandeen, 1970). Such communities believed that the 'Rapture' could happen at any time so one had to be prepared. Additionally how one conducted one's life and what one believed was a pressing concern; everyday belief and conduct became paramount (Sandeen, 1970). These revivalist trends produced a by-product that would become important for the future development of Protestant fundamentalism; they produced pre-formed, loose groupings of conservative Protestants with shared views and beliefs (Sandeen, 1970, Marsden 1980, Ammerman, 1991). These revivals also helped to popularise a number of preachers who would become well known and serve as figure heads for early gatherings of like-minded conservatives. Revivalism was a populist form of Protestantism and revival meetings drew large crowds in the western and northern states. These revival meetings became venues for initial meetings of concerned conservatives who feared that theological trends such as the rejection of literalism, as well as wider social changes would 'corrupt' their absolutist and literal interpretation of faith: the faith that they saw as the 'true' faith. Protestant fundamentalism grew out of these revivalist gatherings (Sandeen, 1970, Marsden 1980, Ammerman, 1991). However, theological concerns were not the only catalyst for the emergence of Protestant fundamentalism.

The End of the 'Empire'

Although it could be argued that, a Protestant hegemony remained in the USA into the twentieth century, with power and institutions still dominated by White, Protestants; Protestants themselves began to perceive themselves to be under threat.

Their 'Protestant Empire' was directly challenged by the biggest mass migration in history, which saw over seventeen million immigrants settle in the USA between 1870 and 1920 (Ahlstrom, 1975). These waves of migration were controversial as eastern and southern Europeans, who were predominantly Catholic or Jewish, dominated them. Catholics had represented around five per cent of the pre-Civil War population; most migrants prior to the Civil War had been northern European Protestants (Ahlstrom, 1975). America's cultural identity appeared under threat from 'foreigners' with 'alien' beliefs and cultures. Conservative Protestants, drawing on their national creation myths, particularly saw this as a 'dilution' of the 'true' American national character; they increasingly saw this in a dualistic manner, with 'true' Americans on one side and 'foreigners' on the other (Scott, 2001). This view of immigrants was compounded by wider social changes that intrinsically linked immigrants to social change.

Modernisation involves a series of inter-related socio-economic and cultural processes that dramatically alter the structure of societies. Modernisation moved through Western Europe, driven by industrialisation, in the late eighteenth and early nineteenth centuries. The USA modernised economically and structurally almost a century later. The USA underwent rapid industrialisation and urbanisation in the post-Civil War era, specifically in the northern states. The South remained predominantly an agrarian economy, which did not significantly industrialise until the post Second World War era. It is therefore not surprising that the conservative Protestantism, from which fundamentalism would emerge, was centred, initially, in the urban, northeastern states, where social and theological changes would have the most impact (Marsden 1980, Ammerman, 1991). Southern fundamentalism would emerge later, in the early twentieth century as social change came later to that region.

Industrialisation brings with it a series of related structural changes to society; it places capitalism at the ideological heart of society, making the pursuit of profit and the consumption of goods, cultural preoccupations. This is the antithesis of most religious sensibilities, which shun materialism as a thing in itself and particularly in the Christian tradition; the pursuit of love of money has always been problematic. The New Testament, in particular, associates poverty with piety and views wealth as a possible hindrance to salvation (Weber, 1992). Capitalism creates increasing divides between social groups, based on wealth, property ownership, skills, and occupation. Such divides can polarise societies into 'haves' and 'have-nots', the latter often feeling marginalised and alienated from the mainstream. Industrialising societies need a steady supply of cheap labour, which often results in high levels of immigration, as immigrants will typically accept reduced wages and poorer working conditions in comparison to 'native' born workers; this was certainly the case in the USA, where the steady waves of immigrants from eastern and southern Europe provided a constant stream of cheap workers. However, immigration brings with it heterogeneity and cultural diversity, which can threaten indigenous communities that may already feel embattled by social change; again we see this in relation to the growth of Protestant fundamentalism in the USA (Bruce, 2002). Industrialisation and immigration in turn fuel urbanisation, the rapid growth of cities; as workers migrate towards those areas (usually urban) where work is readily available. Rapid urbanisation brings with it infrastructural breakdown, poverty, poor housing, increased crime and ill health. In the USA, northern Cities were perceived to be overwhelmed by immigrants; a perception that had some root in reality. For example in 1890, 80 per cent of New Yorkers were foreign born or the children of foreign born parents (Gibson and Lennon, 1999). Such immigrants were viewed as the cause of most urban problems from crime to disease. This is the origin of the prevailing view among fundamentalists today that urban centres, like New York, are 'evil' and 'polluting'. In relation to this is the over-idealisation of rural communities as 'safe' and sanctuaries of the 'true' America (Noll, 1992). Urban areas are by their nature places where people come together but also are alienating places, where individuals and communities can feel dislocated from society and their culture. Thus, cities can become focal points for social movements; again, we see this in the case of religious fundamentalism in the USA, but also across the world. For example, Islamic fundamentalism in the Middle East grew, and remains strong in urban centres, such as Cairo, Tehran, and Istanbul (Bruce, 2008).

The shift into modernity brings with it a changing of cultural views: science and empiricism becomes the default meaning provider. The idea of 'the new' or progress, is embraced and traditions decline, this is facilitated by the adoption of consumerism, which demands a preoccupation with the 'next big thing'. The shift to city living also disrupts traditional practices and beliefs, which were deeply embedded in rural communities; it is harder to maintain such patterns in the heterogeneity of the city, where communities might be dispersed. Individualism as opposed to communalism is embraced in modernity, with the rights of the individual becoming increasingly important (Bruce, 2001 and 2002, Callinicos, 2007). Capitalism and its incumbent division of labour pits individuals against each other in competition but also allows individuals to potentially take control of their own destinies; if one has the right skills and earns enough, one can ascend the social ladder. This challenges religious views of a fixed social order, where God controls the destiny of individuals (Berger, 1967). In modern societies, the individual can literally take control of one's own life, free of traditions that stress fixivity and ascribed status. Urban life, again, emphasises individualism over communalism. Finally, modernisation brings with it secularisation; religions, typically, thrive on communalism, traditions, faith based knowledge, homogeneity, and often fixed social orders. Therefore, modern, urban, individualistic, consumer driven societies are problematic for religions; typically, religion shifts from being a central part of that society to a matter of private belief (Wilson, 1966, Bruce, 2001). Although, as we have noted previously, the USA was established as a secular state and so therefore secularisation as a process of modernisation has not had the impact that can be seen in Western Europe, where churches went into decline. However, secularisation is not just about a decline in participation, but also implies an embracing of secular values and a shift towards moral and cultural plurality; all of which are problematic for religious groups.

However, as religious fundamentalism demonstrates in both the USA and elsewhere, modernisation is both a good and a bad thing for religious communities. Clearly, the shift towards capitalism, consumerism, urban living, and so forth destablises the bases on which religious communities are usually built, such as rural living, homogeneity, tradition and so forth. Yet, those same processes of urbanisation, consumerism and capitalism and so on, have the potential to create groups of disaffected and marginalised individuals unhappy with how their society has changed or at least how they perceive it to have changed (Scott Jones, 2009). Modernisation often happens very quickly so that change can seem very sudden and this can disorient communities. The decline in traditions and religion can further disorient, as they are often the sources of stability, cohesion and identity for individuals and communities (Ter Haar, 2003). Such communities can feel left out of the benefits of social change and can feel that their very culture (and indeed identity) is under threat. These urban populations of the disaffected can be drawn into a variety of social movements, including religious ones. This is the environment where religious fundamentalism prospers as it offers a worldview that draws on traditional patterns of belief, appears to speak to people's cultural heritage, is communalistic in orientation, and provides a critique, based on religion, of modern life (Marty and Appleby, 1994). This is the environment from which Protestant fundamentalism emerged in the latter half of the nineteenth century.

By the 1890s, the USA was increasingly, a culturally and religiously diverse society; that was urban, industrial, scientifically advanced, riven with social inequalities and a number of 'social ills', such as rising rates of urban crime, which were associated with modernisation. Increasingly conservative Protestants did not recognise the nation as their own, perceiving their national identity to be under threat (Marsden, 1980, Ammerman, 1991, Scott, 2001). Given that, Protestants also viewed themselves as doubly 'chosen' both as individuals and as Americans (Ahlstrom, 1975); this sense of threat was deeply disturbing and couched in spiritual terms as a threat not just to their way of life but also to God's broader spiritual master plan. The consequences of modernisation therefore supplied a number of catalysts for what would become Protestant fundamentalism. Initially these were centred on theological challenges to conservative views of scripture, literalism and infallibility (Barr, 1977). These theological issues were amplified by wider socio-economic changes, incumbent with modernisation that made conservative Protestant communities feel under threat culturally and religiously. Drawing on a rhetoric of the past, built upon their sense of religico-national identity, they sought to challenge modernisation and over time provide an alternative vision of America.

Back to the 'Fundamentals' of Faith

As noted previously revival meetings afforded opportunities for conservative Protestants to exchange shared ideas and opinions on what they believed and how they might challenge modernity. These meetings created local coalitions of like-minded conservatives that could plug into churches and networks at a national level. Urban revivalism was especially popular; and prominent, well-known, preachers such as Charles G. Finney, Dwight Moody and Billy Sunday would tour urban centres (Sandeen, 1970, Ammerman, 1991). As cities grew due to industrialisation and immigration, they not only offered a steady supply of participants but they also proved emblematic as symbols of what was wrong with modernity and what the consequences of a shift away from 'true' Protestant values and beliefs would be. These urban revivals tapped into Protestant fears regarding urbanisation, immigration and the spread of secular, capitalist values. These preachers targeted alcoholism, big business and Catholic immigrants as 'signs' that American (read here Protestant) moral values and national character were under threat (Noll, 1992, Marsden, 1980). These revivals attracted Protestants from all denominations and backgrounds; the participants shared the view that personal salvation and following the 'true' way were the most important things, irrespective of church affiliation. What would become fundamentalism grew out of these revival movements (Sandeen, 1970).

A sense of an increasingly shared conservative Protestant identity was encouraged by the organisation of prophecy conferences; the most significant of which was the Niagara Bible Conference, first organised in 1875. The Niagara conference became an annual event, but there were also prophecy conferences in New York (1878), Chicago (1886), Boston (1901) and in other north-eastern cities, which remained popular until the 1920s (Sandeen, 1970). Such conferences were hugely popular as they drew crowds from across the nation; the presence of nationally known preachers aiding their success. These conferences featured sermons from leading Bible teachers and preachers; the focus was on exploring the 'truth' of scripture and linking it to doctrine. These conferences soon became a forum for the development of a critique of modernity (and modernist theology) and the construction of a challenge to it, based on scripture. These conferences facilitated an increasing identification of shared beliefs and concerns (Sandeen, 1970, Marsden 1980, 1984).

By the end of the nineteenth century, conservative Protestants were increasingly formalising their shared views and constructing theological challenges to Liberal theology and Biblical Criticism. The stress was on maintaining the 'purity' of what they believed. In 1890, the Niagara Bible Conference endorsed a 'fourteen points' creed that became known as the 'Niagara Creed', which established fourteen key points of faith. These included a belief in the inerrancy of the Bible; a belief in original Sin; a belief that by being 'born again' you will be 'saved'; a belief in a shared community of those who are 'born again'; and a belief that the end of the world is near and linked to the approaching Millennium, an event that will be marked by the restoration of the nation of Israel. The stress on being 'born again', millennialism, apocalypticism and literalism would remain the hallmarks of conservative Protestants in the USA, especially among fundamentalists (Sandeen, 1970, Marsden, 1980, Ammerman, 1991). In the same era Princeton Theological

Seminary became a centre for theological defences of the conservative position, particularly on the issues of inerrancy and orthodoxy of belief, as demonstrated in the work of Charles Hodge and B.B. Warfield. In 1909, Schofield's pre-millennially annotated version of the King James Bible was published and remains a key text for many conservative Protestants and fundamentalists to this day. Then between 1910 and 1915, A.C. Dixon edited his series of twelve pamphlets entitled *The Fundamentals*, which outlined the 'fundamentals' of faith, including Biblical inerrancy and literalism, a belief in the Second Coming of Christ, moral absolutism and other key aspects of conservative belief (Sandeen, 1970, Marsden, 1980, Ammerman, 1991). This series of pamphlets also introduced the label 'fundamentalist', which was readily adopted by many conservatives (Scott, 2001). By 1915, there was an emerging body of literature, which identified and outlined the conservative Protestant position. This early movement was centred on theological positions, which would serve to reinforce the conservative Protestant identity and act as an ideological bulwark against Liberalism and other 'ills' of modernity. Although there were early calls to 'fight back' against the institutions and individuals who spread secularism, this remained a non-political movement at this time.

The end of the nineteenth century also saw the use of the mass media, in the form of mass circulation newspapers and pamphlets, to communicate the increasingly formalised fundamentalist message. Examples of popular titles include the magazine *Truth*, which focused on millennialism, and the newspaper *The Bible Champion*. Such titles served as a means to communicate shared messages on a national level. By the end of the First World War, 'fundamentalism' referred to a specific core of shared beliefs that set 'fundamentalists' increasingly apart from other non-conservative Protestants (Sandeen, 1970, Marsden, 1980, Ammerman, 1991). Although there was an attempt in 1919 to create an organisation that would represent all 'Christian Fundamentals'; it failed to develop and fundamentalists remained in a collection of coalitions, with typically regional identities.

Early Politicisation and Mobilisation

The early fundamentalist movement, although critical of modernity's social ills, rarely entered into political campaigning on social issues. Instead, their preoccupation remained on theological battles (Marsden, 1980). As noted earlier, fundamentalism emerged in response to theology's attempt to accommodate modernism, which occurred against the background of modernisation. Between the end of the First World War and the mid-1920s, fundamentalist coalitions battled with modernists and liberals within their broader denominations, for example, within the northern Baptist and Presbyterian churches. These battles occurred on many fronts from accusations of 'heretical' teaching in seminaries and church schools to concerns about the orthodoxy of missionaries, church newspapers and leaders. Often the result of such battles was the creation of a separate fundamentalist seminary or newspaper in opposition to the liberal one within that denomination (Ammerman, 1991). The stress on orthodoxy and inerrancy meant that fundamentalists struggled to reach any form of theological compromise with their liberal cousins. By the late 1920s, liberals held power in the main Protestant denominational groupings.

There was one key instance of fundamentalists entering into a campaign that went beyond their denominational boundaries; this was the anti-evolutionism campaign of the early 1920s. Evolutionary theory had been one of the numerous aspects of modernism that fundamentalists (and others) had battled with throughout the second half of the nineteenth century. For Biblical literalists, the first chapter of the *Book of Genesis* outlines and explains Creation: God literally created the world in six days. However, the fight against Darwinism had been a theological one (Lienesch, 2007). This changed in 1920 when former Secretary of State and devout Protestant, William Jennings Bryan launched a national crusade against evolutionism. Bryan critiqued evolutionism for two reasons; firstly he saw it as undermining Biblical teaching and secondly, he believed that Social Darwinism promoted conflict; the First World War being, for him, a prime example of this. Anti-evolutionism became a popular national crusade, which drew together not just fundamentalists but participants from other Christian churches. Fundamentalists organised rallies that called for the eradication of a theory that was deemed atheistic and a 'moral danger' to the future of American civilisation. The focus was particularly on the teaching of evolutionism within schools. In twenty states, campaigners introduced bills to ban the teaching of evolution; these failed to be passed in the northern states but there was more success in the South where anti-evolution laws were passed in Tennessee, Louisiana and Mississippi (Lienesch, 2007). The anti-evolution campaign's ultimate test came in 1925 with the infamous Scopes 'Monkey' trial. Tennessee had passed the *Butler Act*, which prohibited teachers in public schools from denying the Biblical account of creation and from teaching that humans evolved from primates. John Scopes, a school teacher in Dayton, Tennessee, was charged on the 25th May 1925 with breaking the law by teaching evolution (Lienesch, 2007). It remains ambiguous as to whether Scopes set out to test the law on his own or whether he was induced by parties unknown. His case became a cause célèbre when the American Civil Liberties Union (ACLU) financially supported his defence and sent in a legal team led by the prominent attorney Clarence Darrow. The prosecution case was conducted by William Jennings Bryan himself. The case became a public battle between modernism and traditionalism; science and religion. Scopes was found guilty but as Marsden (1980: 186) notes 'in the trial by public opinion and the press, it was clear that the twentieth century, the cities, and the universities had won a resounding victory, and that the country, the South, and the fundamentalists were guilty as charged.' The trial resulted in fundamentalist in-fighting and a wider loss of credibility for fundamentalism within Protestant denominations and the wider population (Lienesch, 2007). The trial created and reinforced the stereotype that fundamentalists were anti-modern, backward, anti-science and anti-education. This stereotype would prevail for the next fifty years (Marsden, 1980).

The remaining inter-war years saw fundamentalism reorganising itself and changing its aims. This had been a movement against modernism's influence on theology. Although fundamentalists considered their cultural identity to be under attack, they believed that by fighting back against theological changes they would thus ensure that the spiritually 'pure' churches, that had cast off modernism, would be able to lessen the impact of social changes for wider society. It should also be noted that in a cultural sense the USA began to fully embrace modernist values in the 1920s, so sympathy for a conservative position that emphasised the past and tradition became increasingly irrelevant to the wider population who were in thrall to 'the modern'. Fundamentalists also began to see themselves as separate from others within their denominational groupings; their way was the 'true' way and the rest, for example, liberals, were viewed as 'apostates'. Increasingly the focus was on an identification that American culture was becoming 'anti-Christian', 'godless', and dominated by secular humanism. This was the beginning of fundamentalists rejecting other Christians as kin and a belief that the moral and cultural decay of society was a 'sign' of the forthcoming 'Rapture' and apocalypse (Marsden, 1980, 1984).

Fundamentalism's solution to this 'decay' was to stress a strict way of living and believing that was deemed 'traditional', orthodox and directed by scripture. The fundamentalists began to abandon attempts to reform the liberal wings of their denominations. Instead, fundamentalists chose a path of increasing separatism by establishing their own independent fundamentalist organisations and creating networks of independent fundamentalist groups. Youth organisations were also formed, as were Bible colleges and institutes. The fundamentalist message was disseminated through the use of the mass media, demonstrating the willingness of fundamentalists to utilise the benefits of modern technology; newspapers like *The Sunday School Times* and the *Moody Monthly* were popular nationally. Radio was also used with Charles Fuller's 'Old-Fashioned Revival Hour' highly popular with its mix of old-style music and preaching. Fundamentalists had to buy network radio slots and usually they preferred to buy time on independent stations instead. By the 1940s, there were over ten national programs and hundreds of local ones. The arrival of television in the 1950s further allowed fundamentalist views to be aired and television would become a powerful tool in the following decades (Ammerman, 1991). This inter-war period should be seen as a time of regrouping, reorganising and where fundamentalists began to appreciate that they were on their own and distinctive in their fight against modernity (Marsden, 1980). It is also a time where they established the organisational foundations from which to launch their post war socio-political campaigns and developed the arsenal of weapons, such as the media, which they would later use to great effect.

The final piece of restructuring that occurred at this time that finalised fundamentalist views of themselves as distinct, different and separate, was the split between 'fundamentalists' and 'evangelicals' (Barr, 1977). Prior to the 1940s 'fundamentalist' was a termed which could be applied to a Protestant who stressed the so called 'fundamentals of faith' such as literalism, moral absolutism, creationism, orthodoxy, apocalypticism and so forth. It also implied an individual who sought to challenge and critique modernism in theological and social terms (Barr, 1977). Such individuals might also refer to themselves as 'evangelical' implying a focus on personal faith, the journey to faith, being 'saved' or 'born again' and an adherence Biblical authority. However, by the 1940s the strains within 'fundamentalism' were beginning to emerge between the 'true' fundamentalists and the fundamentalist evangelicals. The central issues were separatism and engagement in the secular world (Marsden, 1980, 1984). The evangelicals within the fundamentalist movement saw separatism as an abandonment of Christ's call to evangelise and spread the Biblical message; that separatism only allowed liberal interpretations of scripture or secular humanism to proliferate. Related to that was the issue of engagement with liberal churches and indeed mainstream society generally. Evangelicals saw this as crucial not only to spread their message of faith but also to reinvigorate the idea of the 'social gospel' as a means for conservative or orthodox believers to offer solutions to social problems. Fundamentalists viewed society (and other churches) as 'corrupt' and irredeemable, evangelicals considered ecumenism possible if it spread God's message and helped to alleviate social problems (Marsden, 1980, 1984). These issues had been a source of tension for some time and by the 1950s, rifts had developed which saw evangelicals split from their fundamentalist brethren. The evangelicals formed associations with other conservative Protestants, such as Pentecostals and Charismatics. Thus by the 1950s what had been a coalition of like-minded Protestants who had seen themselves as the keepers of the 'true' American faith, and then later as defenders of that faith against theological and social modernism, fell apart. Evangelicals, to some extent, sought to work with and accommodate the modern world, while fundamentalists saw separatism as the only plausible position for the 'true' defenders of the faith (Marsden, 1980, 1984).

Post-war Politicisation and Mobilisation

Following the failure of the anti-evolutionism crusade, which culminated in the debacle of the Scopes trial, fundamentalists had avoided political activism or engagement with the wider culture. Instead, they had remained inward looking, building institutions and organisations, which reinforced their worldview. This could be contrasted with their evangelical cousins who launched evangelical and moral crusades, such as those led by Billy Graham, and worked with other churches to spread their gospel message and raise awareness of social problems. However, rapid cultural change in the 1960s would prove a catalyst for the politicisation and mobilisation of fundamentalist Protestants (Ammerman, 1991).

If modernity could be viewed as the era which gave birth to what would become fundamentalism, then late modernity could be seen as the era in which it came of age as a socio-political force. The USA in the post World War Two era, in common with most western nations, underwent a series of social revolutions, which dramatically altered its cultural and political landscape. Although many of these 'revolutions' had their roots in the 1940s and 1950s they had the greatest impact in the 1960s (Ammerman, 1991). Against a backdrop of post-war affluence and a fully formed consumer society, emerged the Civil Rights, Women's Rights, and later Gay Rights movements. These social movements all had at their heart the issue of representation, power, identity and equality. They all challenged the supremacy of white, male, heterosexual society. These movements were both political and social. The post-war generation, the 'Baby Boomers', came of age in the 1960s and readily embraced the new identity and politics, pop culture; and actively challenged traditional ways of believing and doing. The so-called 'counter-culture' was a heady mixture of culture, politics and social issues that all sought to challenge long-standing status quos, concerning race, gender, sexuality, morality, age and class (Tipton, 1984).

As well as raising awareness of issues, these movements also brought about a number of key legislative changes. The *Civil Rights Act* (1964) outlawed racial discrimination in employment, ended segregation in publicly owned facilities, including schools, and offered greater protection to Black voters. This legislation particularly had an impact in the South where segregation was widespread and embedded in southern culture. The Women's Movement made a number of legislative gains including; the *Equal Pay Act* (1963), the *Civil Rights Act* (1964) which outlawed sex discrimination, the *Equal Employment Opportunity Act* (1972) that aimed to remove remaining inequalities in pay, hiring, and the workplace, and the *Pregnancy Discrimination Act* (1978) which protected the jobs of pregnant women. Perhaps most significantly of all the case of *Roe v. Wade* (1973) legalised abortion in the USA. Homosexual sex was decriminalised across the northern, midwestern and western states throughout the 1970s; starting with Illinois in 1962. Only the southern states maintained a prohibition on homosexual sex, until the Supreme Court overruled all remaining legislation in 2003. Other gay civil rights issues have only gained prominence since the 1990s, where laws offering employment and housing equality have been passed. The issue of same-sex unions remains a contentious one, where some states, such as Vermont, recognise and allow same-sex civil unions, while others, such as California, in 2008, have passed laws prohibiting same-sex marriage.

These social movements disrupted long-standing assumptions regarding race, gender and to a lesser extent sexuality. They helped usher in the Sexual Revolution, which was a key aspect of the counter-culture embraced by the 'Baby Boomers'. By the end of the 1960s and into the start of the 1970s, the USA appeared to have embraced cultural and moral plurality. Liberalism dominated popular culture and all institutions associated with traditional patterns of doing, thinking and believing had been thoroughly challenged, critiqued and to an extent rejected. Conservatives generally and in particular conservative Protestants and fundamentalists alike were dismayed at the rapid social and cultural changes; that were seen as direct attacks on the culture and more importantly moral fibre of the nation, and by implication themselves (Ammerman, 1991, Bruce, 2008). White, Protestant culture had been a key target for the counter-culturists, who identified this culture as having held sway over the USA for too long, to the detriment of most of its citizens. However, for conservative Protestants and fundamentalists this was more than just a sense of losing long standing hegemonic control or being stereotyped as 'out of date'; but was viewed as a direct attack on their religious way of life and in turn an attack on their perceived role as 'keepers' of the 'true' America (Lawrence, 1989).

In relation to race, many fundamentalist churches had viewed the races as created separately by God, using Biblical scripture to justify this view. The Civil Rights legislation of the 1960s and the positive discrimination laws that followed in the 1970s and 1980s were seen as challenging this view of racial destiny. Furthermore as the USA was seen as founded by white Protestants, the granting of equal civil rights to non-white Americans was problematic to some fundamentalists. However, most significantly of all the Civil Rights legislation was seen as over-turning long-standing traditional patterns of life in the South, where segregation had been deeply embedded in the culture. This happened at a time when the South was shifting into the industrial, urban age; by the 1960s the majority of southerners lived in cities and the industrial base had expanded, bringing with it migration from other parts of the country (Ammerman, 1991). The South began to experience the issues of urbanisation and cultural plurality that the northern states had been dealing with since the late nineteenth century. This meant that the South became a key growth area for conservative Protestantism and in particular fundamentalism, whose message reassured that social change could be resisted, over-turned and replaced through embracing the 'fundamentals of faith'.

The changing position of women was viewed by conservatives as problematic due to their belief in gender roles based on scripture; man was made to lead and provide for his family (Bendroth, 1994). Gender laws empowering women and facilitating their shift into the workplace were seen to go against this divine gender scheme, where women were expected to be dutiful, submissive wives and find fulfilment through being mothers. The decriminalisation of homosexual sex and abortion were seen as signs of the moral decay of the USA; the Bible expressly condemns homosexuality and the taking of life. In passing such legislation, the federal government was increasingly viewed as in the hold of the progressive, liberal, secularists and not to be trusted (Carpenter, 1997). The passing of laws, such as the 1963 prohibition on prayers in public schools further implied that federal government no longer had the interests of conservatives at heart and particularly not those who held any religious convictions (Marty and Appleby, 1994).

Fighting for the Soul of America

The changes ushered in by the 1960s were seen by conservatives and fundamentalists in particular, as direct attacks on their way of life, identity and belief system (see for example, LaHaye, 1980). The nation was viewed as in the grip of people who sought to interfere with women's God-ordained role, as stated in the Bible; to grant equal, civil rights to individuals who were 'immoral', such as homosexuals; who sanctioned the 'murder' of innocent children through abortion; and finally, who undermined family life and moral health via the promotion of sex education, free contraception, abortion, and easier divorces. The response was to mobilise and fight back (Carpenter, 1997). Whereas the 1920s and 1930s had been an era of theological battles concerning the future of Protestantism; the 1970s onwards was an era of socio-political battles concerning the future of America.

Fundamentalists had spent the period from the 1940s to the 1970s in separation from other conservative Protestants and out of the mainstream political arena. They had been busy setting up their own schools, colleges, media and so forth. The election of Jimmy Carter, a Southern Baptist, in 1976 was partly due to the mobilisation of southern conservative Protestants who had been coming together around family issues, such as abortion. Although Carter's election caught the press by surprise and led to the belief that conservative, religious communities had greater influence than ever imagined; Carter was soon revealed as a secularist in the political sphere (Ammerman, 1993). By the late 1970s conservative religious groups, including fundamentalists, were campaigning against Carter and coming to the realisation that if they wanted change then they would have to form social networks across theological divides (Carpenter, 1997). Fundamentalists had until the late 1970s existed in a form of splendid isolation from their former evangelical brethren, critical of evangelicals and other conservative Protestants for ecumenism and engagement with secular (and often liberal) society. However the failure of the Carter administration to put conservative protestant issues and values back into the heart of government made evangelicals and fundamentalists alike realise that if they wanted change then they would have to work together and mobilise (Harding, 2000). For fundamentalists it was the acknowledgement that despite theological divisions with other conservative Christians, there were common foes that they all shared. Additionally was the appreciation that by creating alliances they could draw on a large population of disaffected Protestants, with already established networks that could easily be mobilised (Carpenter, 1997). The main networks and organisations were the Moral Majority led by Jerry Falwell, the Religious Roundtable and the American Coalition for Traditional Values. These networks mobilised evangelicals and fundamentalists alike through their stress on moral issues, the key role of conservative religion as a 'cure' for moral decay, and the need to battle for the very 'soul' of America (Bruce, 2008). These groups were established through the existing networks of independent conservative and fundamentalist churches and their incumbent schools, newspapers and so forth. Television had been well used by evangelicals and fundamentalists alike through the post-war era to promote their message and raise funds and was now used to promote these new organisations. These networks deliberately presented themselves as politically non-partisan, thus offering a broad appeal and avoiding becoming mired in political in-fighting. Instead they offered a positive message that the USA could be 'saved' through the reassertion of traditional, Christian (read here Protestant) values that would seek to eradicate those forces and structures that had led it astray (Harding, 2000). This message proved popular beyond religious communities as it tapped into a sense of national decay and decline, in economic, global and social terms. This decline had started with the debacle of the Vietnam War and the shame of Watergate and ended with the economic recession of the late 1970s; groups like the Moral Majority tapped into wider anxieties regarding national decline and linked it to moral and religious decline also (Ammerman, 1991). For believers, particularly fundamentalists, the sense of national decay fed into long standing apocalyptic beliefs, anticipating an 'end of days' (Scott, 2001).

The press soon labelled these newly emerging political networks as the 'New Christian Right'. Through the 1980s organisations, like the Moral Majority, were politically active at all levels; recognising the power of money, they raised vast sums of funds for political campaigns. They also utilised a range of political strategies from direct action, voter registration, leafleting and getting their people elected in to positions of influence at regional and state levels. They reached out beyond their heartlands of evangelical and fundamentalist Protestantism to Americans who felt a sense of national decline and found a reassertion of traditional values appealing (Bruce, 1988). President Reagan's elections of 1980 and 1984 were partly due to the fund raising and campaigning of these groups and Reagan deliberately courted the 'New Christian Right'. He invoked many of their ideals and aims in his presidential campaigns but to an extent, they failed to establish ground at the heart of federal government (Bruce, 1988). Similarly, President George H.W. Bush also courted this bloc of voters but failed to pass legislation that they would see as significant. However, the media and political focus upon them certainly showed that they had arrived as a socio-political force.

The 'New Christian Right' had a range of political successes through the 1980s, particularly at regional and state levels. Nevertheless, they failed to make a significant impact at a national level (Bruce, 1988). However, they can claim to have placed conservative (and fundamentalist) Protestant issues at the heart of political and cultural debate. This can be seen in the increasing gulf between voters in the USA, where a middle ground seems increasingly hard to discern. More importantly, perhaps, at a cultural level, conservative religious values, particularly on moral issues, became highly influential and led to the divisive 'culture wars' of the late 1980s and 1990s (Hunter, 1992). In parallel to the increasing polarity of political opinion in the USA, was the emergence of a clash between liberal secularism and conservative Protestantism at a cultural level, which was played out in popular culture and the arts. At the heart of the 'culture wars' was the issue of morality; what is and is not American; what are the limits on freedom of speech; and what constitutes censorship. The 'culture wars' have, ultimately, been won by the liberals as demonstrated by the increasing liberalisation of television and film, particularly around depictions of homosexuality, gender and sex. The legacy of the 'culture wars' is an appreciation by conservatives of the importance of culture as an arena for political campaigning and also publicity.

The Clinton era saw some decline in support for the 'New Christian Right' but it also served to rally the forces of conservative religion around a new political target. The Clinton administration was viewed as particularly 'corrupt' and ultra-liberal. The 'New Christian Right' successfully mobilised to aid the election of President George W. Bush. The closeness of the presidential election in 2000 demonstrated the national political divide between red and blue states; red states being dominated by religious conservatives. The election of Barack Obama in 2008 has already provided the politicised religious conservatives with a political target who is seen as even more liberal and 'left wing' than President Clinton and should prove a catalyst for further politicisation given his commitment to legally recognise same-sex civil unions, to over-turn the 'don't ask, don't tell' rule on gays in the military, and to develop an effective public health system. Chapter 8 of this book will explore fundamentalist political campaigning in more detail.

Contextualising God's Way Community

As God's Way community serve as the key case study in this book it is relevant to briefly discuss their place in this wider historical context. Abraham Zion, their founder, was born and raised in St Louis, Missouri at the end of the nineteenth century. His family were Methodists who were 'born again' and involved in church missions to the poor in the growing city. As a child and adolescent, Abraham was immersed in evangelical debates regarding the impact of modernity on American society, particularly with regard to urbanisation, immigration and secularism. However he left home when he became disaffected with his family's (and church's) focus on social mission work, rather than on reasserting core values. Abraham travelled extensively throughout the south-western states, experiencing 'frontier' forms of Protestantism, while also absorbing the growing literature emerging from the early fundamentalist movements in the north-eastern states. By young adulthood he had set up his own small religious community, which he led based on a series of divine revelations that led him to feel 'chosen' (Scott, 1996). A feeling beyond 'just' being 'born again' to appreciate the power of scripture, but rather a feeling that he was on a personal mission directed by God. Following the establishment of God's Way community in southern Missouri in 1935, Abraham focused on a strategy of isolation, precipitated by growing unease with wider social changes and by the failure of fundamentalist churches to bring about change. However the social revolutions of the 1960s impacted on the community and ultimately led to a schism between those members who wished to embrace the outside world, where it might benefit them in terms of economic prosperity, and those members who believed that 'letting in' the secular was leading to a corruption of their founding values.

The schism of the 1970s left a smaller community, led by Isaac Zion, Abraham's eldest son, but one that viewed itself as having been 'tested' by God for embracing some elements of the secular. From the 1970s onwards, the community adopted a strategy of isolation until it began to see the potential power of working in wider local networks for change on issues relating to the power of federal government, home schooling, abortion and the decline in the family (Scott, 1996). By the 1990s, there was a wider fundamentalist network that was readily available for them to connect to via the media and many issues with which to become politicised. God's Way's history mirrors the wider history of Protestant fundamentalism; with their origins in the early twentieth century as modernism impacted on American society. Their belief system, demonstrates the creative and fluid nature of American Protestantism (Noll, 1992). Their relationship with other fundamentalists and wider society also mirrors the changing socio-political engagement of the wider fundamentalist community, with its growing awareness that even 'the chosen' may have to work in alliances with those they may not deem as 'true believers'. Chapter 8 will explore God's Way's political activity in more detail.

A Dynamic Demographic

One final point to make concerning the history of fundamentalism and the growth of fundamentalist political action is in regard to demographics. As noted in Chapter 2 polls suggest that a significant number of Americans adhere to beliefs that are the cornerstones of Protestant fundamentalism. However, more importantly for a socio-political movement fundamentalism shows strength in numbers across both sexes, all socio-economic groups and all age groups (Ammerman, 1993). Fundamentalism's heartlands remain the southern and midwestern states; the areas that Ammerman (1993: 8) characterises as 'where tradition is meeting modernity'. In other words, the areas where the battle for the 'soul' of America is still being fought; rather than in urban centres on the west or east coasts where the battle looks lost. However, it should be stressed that this is overwhelmingly a white phenomenon.

Black Protestantism in the USA has developed in separation from white versions; white Protestantism is hegemonic and tied to national identity. Black Protestantism has always been linked to the resistance and empowerment of disadvantaged communities (Noll, 1992). Although Black Protestantism can be deeply conservative on moral issues, it is typically liberal on social issues and Black churches played a key role in shaping and supporting the Civil Rights movement (Noll, 1992). White conservative Protestants, particularly fundamentalists, often maintain racist views particularly in the southern states; thus, Protestant fundamentalism with its concern with White cultural identity and desire to reassert a Protestant hegemony is the antithesis of Black Protestantism, with its concerns for conservative moral values but also wider social equalities. Protestant fundamentalism is an overwhelmingly White phenomenon in the USA.

Chapter 4
'God's Chosen': The Importance of Being 'Chosen'

The previous chapter outlined the history of American Protestant fundamentalism, with its birth within modernity and its growth and entry into the wider political and cultural arena, within the late modern era. To understand fully this history and the political activity of fundamentalists, it is important to explore their worldview and the following chapters seek to do this, drawing predominantly on the God's Way case study (Scott, 1996). A model of the worldview of Protestant fundamentalism was outlined in Chapter 2, which drew on Marty and Appleby's (1991: ix–x) 'family resemblances' model and featured a range of social and theological characteristics. In that chapter, it was argued that the core feature of this worldview was the belief in being 'chosen' and that, a belief in a 'chosen' status was the foundation of the entire worldview. That this belief in being 'chosen' shaped, energised and infused the rest of the worldview. This chapter will explore the idea of 'being chosen' and will argue that without it fundamentalists are not fundamentalists.

The Importance of Being 'Chosen'

Religious and non-religious cultural groups throughout history, including the ancient Jews, the Romans, Victorian English imperialists and of course the Nazis, have made claims to being 'unique', 'special' and indeed a 'chosen' people. It is a recurring ideological device to demarcate a cultural group or set of beliefs as separate from the rest and typically in opposition to competing beliefs. Burkitt (1914) makes the point that the adoption of monotheism and with it the claim to being a 'chosen' people of God set the ancient Jews apart from their polytheistic neighbours. A belief in 'being chosen' or 'special' can serve a range of socio-political needs including, offering resistance (as exemplified by the ancient Jews), legitimising colonisation (as exemplified by the Romans and the Victorian British), justifying opposition and war (as exemplified by the Nazis), as well as reinforcing related beliefs such as racism (as exemplified by the Nazis). When claims to being 'chosen' are also attached to a set of religious beliefs, they become particularly powerful as they add a sense of divine agency to the sense of uniqueness (McGinn, 1984). Politically this makes such groups particularly powerful foes, as they literally believe that they are fighting for God; this can be seen specifically in the case of religious fundamentalists. One final point that should be made with regard to the utility of claims to 'being chosen' is that they can serve as a useful marketing tool to attract potential converts. A group are able to literally claim that 'God is on our side' and therefore we have all the answers; this is an attractive sales pitch, particularly if aimed at individuals who feel isolated and marginalised from mainstream society (Marty and Appleby, 1994).

'Chosen' Status and Communal Identities

Being 'chosen' is both an individual and a communal identity; indeed one might argue that one cannot be a member of a wider community of 'chosen' unless one has experienced the personal revelation of 'being chosen. However, in relation to American Protestantism the communal identity of 'being chosen' creates the historical context for the emergence of the fundamentalist belief in a special status at both a communal and individual level (Ahlstrom, 1975, Ammerman, 1991, Marsden, 1980). As discussed in the previous chapter, American Protestants share a foundation myth that places them, in the figures of the Puritans and specifically the Pilgrim Fathers, at the creation of the USA and intrinsically links their beliefs and values to the national identity.

This also feeds into the wider national identity of the USA as a 'chosen' nation in itself. From its foundation, the USA was built to be an ideal, 'perfect' society, free of the traditions and superstitions that were seen to hold back progress and freedom in Europe (Bloch, 1985). The founders of the USA saw it as having an almost messianic destiny to present a modernist vision of a near utopian society where Enlightenment ideals of justice, equality and freedom were to be celebrated and venerated (Bloch, 1985). This utopianism is still evident in the idea of the 'American Dream'. The USA's view of itself as 'different', 'new' and 'special' led to a national sense of agency that is still evident in American foreign policy to this day: that is the USA has a special responsibility to encourage democracy and uphold freedoms around the world. One might argue that a sense of 'chosen' status is embedded within the American national character and polity (Bloch, 1985, Ahlstrom, 1975). The American Protestant identity therefore featured a heady blend of national destiny and agency which identified (White) Protestants as special 'guardians' of this destiny due to their status as the authentic 'true' Americans. This sense of special status remained unarticulated until the end of the nineteenth century; as the majority of the population were white Protestants and therefore there was no need to demarcate some Americans as more 'authentic' than others. However this 'Protestant empire' began to fall apart by the end of the nineteenth century with the shift into modernity, bringing with it incumbent challenges to the White protestant hegemony (Scott, 2001).

The rise in Protestant fundamentalism was precipitated by a reaction to modernisation. However, this was a reaction due to a perception of cultural attack on the USA itself and Protestants specifically. In other words the identification of White Protestants as 'true' Americans and guardians of the national destiny, which had lain dormant for a century, suddenly became articulated by communities that perceived themselves to be 'under threat' and who believed themselves to be tasked with protecting the national character. Thus, a sense of 'being chosen' is embedded deeply within American Protestantism in relation to both a national and a religico-cultural identity. The fundamentalist 'solution' to modernisation was to reassert core or 'fundamental' beliefs and values that looked back to their Protestant heritage and that were articulated as 'authentic' beliefs both culturally and religiously (Marsden, 1980). The stress on core values like literalism, scriptural inerrancy and moral absolutism, rely on claims to 'being chosen' for validation. After all why accept that the Bible is the absolute word of God or other such views unless you can be sure that the purveyors of that view are themselves 'special' and authentic in some way. Thus, a sense of 'calling' and 'being chosen' that were already part of a religico-cultural identity was further validated and reinforced by a specific theological challenge to modernism. By drawing on rhetoric of an imagined past, fundamentalists could invoke a sense of special status, that was further validated by theological beliefs (Harding, 2000). Fundamentalists' invocation of the idea of a special status, linked to a national and religious identity under threat, was also a useful means to articulate the disparate and complex social issues involved in modernisation. They were able to present a clear and simple message that was readily understandable and appealing to a broad mass of people who felt buffeted by social change: modernity is threatening the soul of the USA and by implication the way of life of the 'true' Americans (i.e. White, Protestants). Thus the emerging Protestant fundamentalist communities of the late nineteenth century considered themselves as 'special', 'unique' and a 'chosen' people; 'chosen' to save the soul of the USA (Marsden, 1980). This view remains a key aspect of fundamentalist political rhetoric today.

'Chosen' Status and Personal Identities

Protestantism places personal experience at its heart; one key aim of the Protestant Reformation was to strip away the barriers that existed between the individual and God (Lindberg, 2005). To varying degrees, all forms of Protestantism lay an emphasis on the means to gain personal salvation, an exemplified by the translation of the Bible into the vernacular and the abandonment of church hierarchies of power. Non-conformist Protestantism particularly places emphasis on the individual's encounter with God and the importance of realising that encounter in everyday life. Non-conformism embraces direct encounter with God, whether through embodied experiences (for example, glossalia, trance, or dance) or through mental experiences (for example, dreams, signs and symbols). As was noted in the previous chapter, American Protestantism has a history of non-conformism and eclecticism (Noll, 1992). The lack of institutionalised Protestantism and denominationalism inevitably resulted in an emphasis in American Protestantism on personal experience with the divine. Liberal Protestants downplayed personal faith encounters as outdated and anti-modern and focused instead on the social gospel and scripture as allegory. Conservative Protestants, including fundamentalists, drew on the power of the personal faith encounter to validate their positions on literalism and absolutism. A sense of personal encounter with God, whether described as becoming 'born again' or 'being chosen' was important to link that individual to the wider rhetoric of a 'chosen' people with a special national destiny. Personal testimony of the divine was a key feature of Biblical Prophecy conferences and other gatherings of fundamentalists, reinforcing a sense of 'mission' and 'rightness' (Ammerman, 1991). It remains a staple of the fundamentalist and evangelical media today (Harding, 2000).

The Construction of a 'Chosen' Status

Obviously within each specific community 'chosen' status, both personal and communal may develop and be expressed differently within the broader stream of Protestant fundamentalism. It is useful to explore how a specific community can come to view themselves as 'chosen' via the direction of their leader, as was the case with God's Way community. Abraham Zion, the founder of God's Way community, is a typical charismatic leader (Gerth and Mills, 1991, Kanter, 1973) around which the community coalesced. Abraham's personal encounters with God led to the creation of the community and served to shape its development. He remains a communal figurehead almost forty years after his death. Abraham grew up in a Methodist family committed to mission work in the poor areas of the city of St Louis[1]. He was influenced in his adolescence, via newspapers and other conservative publications, by the growing fundamentalist movement that was spreading through the Northeastern states in the late nineteenth century. By his late adolescence, Abraham had left home, disaffected by the 'social gospel' work of his family and seeking a more 'authentic' version of faith. He considered 'social gospel' work as less important than the need to 'save' the Gospel in the first instance, viewing it as under threat. His early experiences working in the poor areas of St Louis, which were teeming with European immigrants, predominantly Catholics, validated what he read in conservative and fundamentalist newspapers of the 'threat' to the nation's religious and therefore national character. The members of God's Way community still recount stories Abraham used to tell about the poverty, depravity and other social evils of the city, which feature Catholic immigrants (the 'non-believers') as the key players in the decline of St Louis from a 'pretty American town' to a 'city of the damned'.

Abraham travelled through the American southwest where he experienced being 'born again' and became involved in revival camp gatherings where he was influenced by a variety of different preachers who discussed the popular fundamentalist beliefs that were spreading in the northeastern states. He started preaching at these camp revivals and gathered a small group of followers around

1   All material relating to God's Way community from Scott, 1996.

him. He believed that America was 'under attack' and entering a period of moral decline that would culminate in the end of the world as foretold in the Bible. Abraham preached that 'true' believers needed to come together and ready themselves for the final confrontation between the forces of good and evil that would soon come. Following a snakebite-induced coma, he started to believe that he and his followers in particular were uniquely 'chosen' above all others. Abraham claimed that while in his coma he had experienced a series of visions from God, including a terrifying vision of the end of the world. In his visions, God had 'called' Abraham to lead 'the chosen' and found a community where they could live and ready themselves for the end of the world. Abraham had been shown by God that his community alone would survive the end of the world and live on in the coming 'Heaven on Earth'. This led him to establish the original God's Way community in Arizona, with a small band of followers who believed that God had 'chosen' Abraham to lead them and that through him they were all 'chosen'. This original community failed but another series of visions led Abraham in 1935 to move his community to the Midwest, where God had 'told' him they would be led to a 'chosen' land where they would prosper; 'signs' would be 'given' on their journey to show them the way and to identify their final resting place. When they eventually established their new settlement, it was deemed to be on sacred land, 'chosen' by God and various 'signs' had been read to tell them this was the 'right' place. Thus, the very land that the community is built on is seen as 'chosen' by God for the 'chosen'; they view it as having 'special' properties including a particularly rich growing soil ('our crops never fail') and especially pure drinking water that is deemed to have healing and cleansing properties. When ill, members would only drink the water in the belief that it alone would heal whatever ailed them.

Abraham's early biography shows that he had been clearly influenced by and believed in the turn of the century, fundamentalist position on faith, morality and social change. He had actively spread the fundamentalist message in his own preaching; using his personal experience of 'being chosen' to validate what he preached. His establishment of a community of believers is in keeping with the isolationist and retreatist tendencies of inter-war Protestant fundamentalism (Barr, 1977, Marsden, 1980). The community was to be a haven for 'the chosen' and an example of the 'right' way to live for other Protestants who might be encouraged to join. Through following Abraham and living communally his followers achieved 'chosen' status.

The community, during its early years maintained little direct contact with other fundamentalist groups, preferring to focus on their own particular version of faith. During these isolationist years the community further developed its view of its own uniqueness, and this led them to shun any attempts at proselytising or outreach work with other fundamentalist Protestants. Isolationism is a common strategy utilised by social groups who believe that they are 'chosen' by God (Burkitt, 1914). This view had been encouraged by their near isolationist position and by Abraham's further divine visions, which informed him not to 'trust' fully any version of the Bible as it had been edited so many times, particularly by the

Catholic Church; instead, the community were to draw on a series of scriptures that God dictated to Abraham via his visions. These scriptures, which are bound together and called the *Books of Abraham* are a loose collection of sayings, songs, and obscure writings and is in of two volumes. One volume consists solely of songs, which are used in worship and during everyday communal tasks, while the other is more scripture focused. The Bible was not rejected outright – the *Old Testament* was seen as largely unrevised and therefore the literal 'word' of God; its use as a sacred text by Jews, God's 'original' 'chosen' further validated this view. However, the *New Testament* was seen as 'corrupted' by successive translators and churches, and therefore was seen as less reliable. The community draw heavily on the *Old Testament* and the *Books of Abraham* for worship and daily guidance.

However, by the 1960s the community's isolationist position was preventing it from growing, as it was unable to directly seek out new members. A lack of population growth is a common problem for all groups that adopt an isolationist position: how do they reproduce the next generation and maintain the community's development, typically when existing kinships ties amongst founding members prevent intra-marriage (Kanter, 1972, 1973). Abraham's solution to this problem was to 'open' up the community to the 'outside' through preaching the community's message to the local community, as well as joining local networks of like-minded fundamentalists, for example, through sending the community's children to a local fundamentalist run school. This tentative participation in a wider fundamentalist community resulted in considerable growth for God's Way and by the mid-1960s, due to a steady stream of new members, and at its peak it had a population over one hundred and fifty. This strategy of engagement with the wider community had been successful in terms of bringing in new members but it also opened up the community to external influences.

The community's younger generation, having experienced external schooling, were exposed to the messages of the wider popular culture 'revolutions' of the 1960s and were challenging many of their elders' beliefs. The size of the community and its participation in wider faith-based networks led to the emergence of competing views of their faith and 'chosen' status, with some members wishing to view all Protestants who were like them as 'chosen', whether they lived on the community or not. Other members wished to retain their claims to uniqueness and lessen their participation in external networks. A central issue concerned the issue of 'fighting back' against those forces deemed to be 'corrupting' America; should the community retreat into isolation and view everything as 'lost' or should they seek to fight alongside others who shared many of their key views? This tension between isolationism and participation in the secular world is a tension that has existed within the Protestant fundamentalist movement since the 1940s (Marsden, 1980, Ammerman 1991, Carpenter, 1997). Underpinning this was the issue of what God would want them to do and Abraham had not had any 'signs' from God since the early days of their foundation. These issues were contained through Abraham's leadership and the community's deference to him. However, by the early 1970s, as

Abraham's health failed, the tensions over the community's direction and view of themselves exploded and culminated in a schism.

The community were divided into three groups; a small group who wanted to leave and live in mainstream secular society; and two large groups each led by one of Abraham's two sons. One son, Joshua Zion, took a large group away to found a new community, which would be completely isolationist and would await the end of the world as the 'true chosen'. Joshua's group still live today, in splendid isolation, somewhere in Washington State. The other group, led by Isaac Zion, would remain on the original community and seek a path that encouraged working within wider social networks in order to 'fight back'. Isaac's group still maintained a view of themselves as 'chosen' but believed that through wider engagement they might attract new members and do 'God's work' while awaiting their apocalyptic destiny. This divergence between Abraham's two sons centres on their interpretation of 'being chosen' and of the end of the world. One sees it as imminent and therefore the 'chosen' can do nothing but live 'correctly' and wait; while the other sees it as 'close' and that the 'chosen' must show themselves to be 'true soldiers' of God by rallying new members and demonstrating their ability to fight for God. The community today is still led by Isaac Zion and has a small membership of thirty-seven; they have not been very successful at attracting new members, but they still maintain that they alone are 'chosen' by God and will live on after the end of the world.

The Reinforcement and Maintenance of 'Being Chosen'

The long-term existence of any religious worldview is problematic as its socially constructed nature always threatens to be revealed (Berger, 1967). Thus, the need to hide the 'hand of man' is a constant issue; there must be structures and activities in place that mystify and legitimise the belief system. The wider secularisation of western societies place particular pressure on religious mystification structures, as they are built on faith-based knowledge that cannot withstand empirical scrutiny (Bruce, 2002). Thus the need to reinforce and maintain any religious worldview is important; its claims to truth must constantly be articulated, demonstrated and validated through the everyday activities of believers. Another issue is that religious worldviews often make extraordinary claims that may set a worldview up to 'fail' (Festinger et al., 1964, Berger, 1967). An example would be a belief in a set date for the end of the world; when that date passes, a group must find a way to account for the failure of their worldview, which simultaneously reinforces and validates it further. If they fail to do this then the group will experience 'meaning crisis' and soon begin to question their belief system further, perhaps to the point, where the group is no longer sustainable (Festinger et al., 1964).

Long established religions or groups within a particular religion, have a number of devices by which they can reinforce and maintain their worldviews: the power of history lends authenticity and cultural cache to beliefs, usually offering a high degree of social legitimacy (McGuire, 1997). A range of socialisation mechanisms transmit beliefs down through the generations, while an array of rituals operate to direct the individual and community through the life course allowing an instrumental focus (Berger, 1967). Finally scriptures and scriptural authorities (for example, priests) offer textual (and usually historic) support for views. Newer religions or religious communities lack much of this arsenal of mystification and legitimation, hence the high levels of public scepticism and distrust towards new religious movements. Such communities particularly must have strong mechanisms in place to reinforce and maintain their worldviews (Kanter, 1972). God's Way is such a community and one that claims that it alone is 'chosen' by God: quite a claim for thirty-seven people living in the rural Midwest of the USA.

The community have a range of structures in place that facilitate the reinforcement and maintenance of their worldview. Firstly, they are able to draw on a sense of a shared American (White) Protestant identity that links them to a wider historical heritage that they can draw upon: a heritage that gives them a sense of being 'true' Americans. They are highly patriotic, demonstrated by their support of soldiers and veterans' organisations (some members are veterans). They participate in national secular rituals like Thanksgiving and Independence Day (both events they see as associated with 'True' Americans' i.e. White Protestants), and they fly of the American flag on their land. Yet they are highly critical of the federal government, which they see as corrupt and dominated by the 'non-believers'. They also criticise revisionist attempts to downplay foundation myths like Thanksgiving or to make them more culturally inclusive. Secondly, they can draw on a shared Protestant fundamentalist identity that they inherited through Abraham's identification with fundamentalism and through their wider participation in local fundamentalist networks. The community send their children to a local fundamentalist school; they listen to Christian radio, read several conservative Christian newspapers, and donate money to local fundamentalist political campaigns. They occasionally attend prophecy meetings in the local community. More importantly, their worldview is built on many beliefs that are shared with the wider Protestant fundamentalist community: scriptural literalism, moral absolutism, a stress on orthodoxy and orthopraxy, and apocalypticism (Barr, 1977, Ammerman, 1991). Their particular enactment of these belief positions is of course shaped by their specific history and view of their own 'chosen' status.

However, their sense of being uniquely 'chosen' draws most heavily on their shared communal history, particularly in relation to the figure of Abraham Zion. Abraham's charismatic leadership brought them together and kept them together, proving him 'special'. However, it is his experience of divine revelations that are especially important in the constructing, reinforcing and maintaining of their view in a special identity that marks them out from others like them and that establishes their future destiny. In turn, this sense of destiny validates how and why they live as they do. It is therefore no surprise that stories of Abraham's life abound in daily communal life ('Abraham would see it this way....' or 'Abraham did this....');

he is a figurehead and a symbolic device for validating and reinforcing their view of themselves. His journey is their journey, his experiences the source of their identity.

The physical environment of the community is also deemed 'chosen', a sacred, special place: 'given' by God to the community, a 'chosen' land that was foretold to Abraham. Thus, the mere act of living on this land facilitates their communal sense of being 'chosen'. The land's special status is reinforced through the view that anything can grow on it (although in reality this is not actually the case) and what does grow, grows in abundance. The food that they grow is deemed particularly nutritious and the water from their well is seen as exceptionally pure, with the power to heal. When members are ill they will only drink communal well water, in the belief that it will cure anything. Similarly, when washing clothes or dishes, no soap detergent is used as the well water is seen to be such a powerful cleanser: this results in food encrusted dishes and soiled clothes of which the community's members seem oblivious. Their view of the physical space as sacred is also reinforced through the saying of a protection prayer on exiting and a thanksgiving prayer on re-entry; illustrating their separation of sacred and profane space. Their land is surrounded by a fence and along with the existence of a manned watchtower, further reinforces the view of separation and 'specialness'. Because the land is deemed sacred the community's members view all activity on the community as sacred; from formal religious worship to the act of sweeping the floor. Thus, all activities are conducted in a ritualised, reverent style.

For example, daily housekeeping activities are done in a set way, accompanied by ritualised sayings (like 'God sees dust') or songs; they are acts of worship in themselves. Through maintaining the physical space, the members are helping to maintain their spiritual identity. A focus on instrumental tasks is a useful device for reinforcing any belief system and thus God's Way community stress the importance of constant activity: everything must be purposeful. This mania for occupation can be seen in the fact that even when ill, members seek to 'keep busy'. Leisure activities usually involved purpose, such as quilting, carpentry, and even watching television for the adults involved only watching programmes that focused on their spiritual beliefs. The stress on activity links to their belief in 'being chosen': 'chosen' status is 'given' and thus can also be removed by God. This means that the community must constantly live up to their status and prove to God that they are worthy of it; through what they do, believe and say. They believe that God is constantly watching them (as articulated through the constant repetition of the phrase 'God sees dust') and judging them as to whether they are truly 'chosen'. This view of being watched constantly by God means that a concern with orthodoxy and orthopraxy dominates. As they consider themselves to be 'chosen' then they presume that their beliefs are the 'right ones' and thus see themselves as 'true' upholders of orthodoxy. In a similar vein how they act out their faith in their everyday lives demonstrates their 'chosen' status but also shapes it in turn; there is a sense of how will God view this behaviour over that behaviour. The community believe themselves to be living the 'right' way (i.e. orthopraxic) but seek validating 'signs' from God in a constant loop that feeds back into behaviour. An example of this in action would be an incident when some of the community's teenagers were caught listening to secular rock music on the radio. This coincided with a small tornado that caused extensive damage to one of the community's buildings; the tornado was taken as a 'sign' of divine displeasure, and this led to a prohibition on all radio listening for the community's teenagers and children. Similarly, a particularly good harvest or the birth of a healthy baby were seen as 'signs' that they were living the 'right' way and that God was rewarding them. Their 'chosen' status was never taken for granted and viewed as something to be worked at and demonstrated at all times. Chapter 5 explores in more detail how orthodoxy and orthopraxy are embedded in communal life.

Another means to reinforce the community's worldview is through its stress on the communal over the individual. Individualism is problematic for small religious groups as it can pose a challenge to communal consensus on what they believe (Kanter, 1972, Hechter, 1987). Most small religious groups, like cults, must find ways to devalue individual experience over communal (Kanter, 1972, Hechter, 1987). God's Way community do this through the design of their buildings; there are several houses that are each shared by a specific family grouping. Such groupings are based on the original founding families (there were five) but most now feature members that are not necessarily related to that founding family. Within each house there are no internal doors, only doorframes, thus wherever you are in the house you can hear and see what other people are doing. The only exception is the bathroom where a curtain can be drawn for modesty but which if drawn for too long engenders curiosity and comment. The houses are used mainly for sleeping and washing in; most communal indoor activity occurs in the communal dining hall and the chapel. All meals are communal events; communally prepared by the community's older women, and eaten by everyone at the same time. The end of each meal sees 'cleaning up' as a shared task. At the start of meals, members hug and greet each other. Children are seen as communal property and disciplined by all adults. Birthdays are celebrated communally on a monthly basis, thus all those born in June have the same birthday celebration; no presents are given. Married couples have their own bedroom, while everyone else shares several to a room. Possessions and clothes are all communally held and shared: thus on washday there is a scramble by the younger members to get the 'best' clothes before someone else gets them. These are all key ways to reinforce a sense of communal identity over individual ones, and can be seen utilised in a wide variety of communal groups, religious and secular (Kanter, 1972, Hechter, 1987).

Their adherence to the belief in scriptural literalism both in relation to the *Old Testament* and the *Books of Abraham* provide a source of doctrinal legitimation that serves to validate and justify their way of life. Scripture is particularly useful in supporting their apocalyptic views and is often used to explain why the end of the world seems to be constantly postponed by drawing on scriptural 'lessons' within the Bible's main apocalyptic writings, such as the *Books of Daniel, Isaiah* and *Ezekiel*. Scripture also legitimises their moral absolutism, which operates in conjunction with a belief in being 'chosen': a belief in moral absolutes requires a strong sense of personal rightness and a belief in being 'chosen' lends itself to a belief in being 'right'. Finally, their belief in being 'chosen' is further constructed and reinforced through their apocalyptic beliefs. Apocalyptic and millenarian beliefs typically work in conjunction with beliefs in being 'chosen', 'special' or 'unique' (Burkitt, 1914, McGinn, 1994). There is an obvious reason for this in that if a group have been established as 'chosen' then it must be for a reason, otherwise why be 'chosen' in the first place. Typically, this divine destiny is linked to views of a future upheaval, conflict, change or ending; thus the group are created with the ultimate aim of inheriting the new social order that follows whatever cataclysmic events are predicted. This sense of a future destiny then operates in a feedback loop with the sense of being 'chosen' that both validates it and reinforces it: we are 'chosen' therefore we have this destiny; we have this destiny because we are 'chosen' (McGinn, 1994). All activity is therefore directed ultimately towards the apocalyptic event and it is made sense of through the belief in being 'chosen'. Maintaining a belief in an imminent ending of the world and a special role within it sets any religious group a challenge: what happens when the predicted world does not end. This can be the ultimate test of a worldview and is particularly problematic when that worldview draws on discourses of being 'chosen' to establish a role within that end of the world scenario. This issue will be explored in more detail in Chapter 6, but God's Way community negotiate this problem by drawing on their sense of personal communication with God: thus particularly bad weather across the USA might be seen as a 'sign' of the beginning of the end. However if that bad weather is then followed by really good weather it is read as a 'sign' that God is just 'testing' people.

Are all 'Chosen', Chosen?

The community might maintain the view that they are the 'chosen' but they view this status as something to be earned and 'given' by God; in other words simply living on their community and participating in their way of life is not sufficient to make you 'chosen'. The community's children and teenagers were not deemed 'chosen' but had a special status as 'vulnerable' with the potential to become 'chosen'. At eighteen, all teenagers could either choose to go through the community's initiation process or leave: none left. The initiation process took a year and involved intensive study of the Bible and the *Books of Abraham*. It also involved the initiate spending long hours in isolation, praying and contemplating. The process ends when the initiate experiences being 'born again' through a divine encounter, whether in a dream, a trance, or in prayer. This personal encounter with God is seen as a 'sign' that the initiate had been deemed worthy of 'chosen' status and can therefore participate fully in the community. This experience is followed by a communal ritual, where the initiate leads the community in worship and recites, from memory, long passages from scripture. Technically, an individual could live on the community without experiencing 'being chosen' but that individual's future destiny would be more problematic in terms of what would happen at the end of the world. All adult members had successfully completed the initiation process and all had experienced a personal encounter with the divine. However, for the community's initiates and teenagers, there was much worry about whether they would experience being 'born again' and this proved to be a useful disciplinary tool for the community's adults who enjoyed reminding the teenagers that all bad behaviour would count against them in God's eyes. All members who finish the initiation process are viewed as equally 'chosen'; there is no sense of hierarchy in relation to 'chosen' status. Although Abraham was seen to have a special relationship with God, he is not seen as any more 'chosen' than the other members, past or present. Similarly, although the community have a strict gender division of labour and a male dominated governance, they do not view men as being more 'chosen' than women. Indeed, most of the community's members view Sarah Zion, Abraham's oldest daughter, as the 'finest ever of God's chosen', due to her humility, work ethic, and grace under pressure.

'Chosen' and 'Fallen'

Cultures and social groups who lay claim to a sense of uniqueness or 'chosen' status, typically, construct an oppositional worldview. That is, they view the world around them as divided into those like themselves and all 'others'. This oppositionality is essential in reinforcing the 'chosen' worldview's authenticity (Burkitt, 1914, Said, 1978). After all, how can one be 'chosen' unless there exists individuals or groups who are not in that category? The 'non-chosen' operate as an 'other' to symbolise all that the 'chosen' are and are not. 'Othering' is a device that reinforces one group's values, identity, norms and so forth, by contrasting them with those that are deemed to belong to another group, whose values are perceived as being opposite and not as good. The 'other' is always what 'we are not', but this 'othering' is a social construction and the 'other' is a repository for stereotypes, stigmatisation and discrimination (Said, 1978). Typically, the 'other' is a subordinate culture or social group whose subordination is reinforced via 'othering'. Periods of colonisation and imperialism are rife with 'othering' and likewise racism is supported by 'othering' (Said, 1978). However, in the oppositionality of the fundamentalist worldview the 'other' is all those who are not classified as 'chosen', thus this is a much more blunt form of 'othering' than usual.

Fundamentalists who view themselves as 'chosen' typically categorise all 'others' as 'fallen' or 'non-believers'. God's Way community used both terms, but the former was most commonly used. The 'fallen' serve a number of purposes in relation to the fundamentalist worldview. Firstly, they reinforce the 'chosen' status of the community. Secondly, they reinforce the community's beliefs, norms and values through contrasting them with those of the 'fallen', which are deemed to be 'immoral, 'evil', 'ungodly' and so forth. To illustrate, while the 'chosen' do not drink alcohol or take drugs, the 'fallen' do; similarly, while the 'chosen' only exist to do God's work, the 'fallen' only exist to undo God's work and so forth. Thirdly, the 'fallen' reinforce the community's apocalyptic beliefs by playing the role of those who will not survive the end of the world and instead face a final divine judgement and punishment; in contrast to the role played by the community. Finally, the 'fallen' exist to provide a range of targets with which to focus the community's (and other fundamentalists') disaffection and anger with mainstream, secular society. Thus helping to focus their critique of secular, modern life, and also providing a range of specific groups and institutions to target in political campaigns. This final point will be explored more fully in Chapter 8.

Fundamentalists typically have a range of those that they categorise as 'fallen', including homosexuals, secularists, liberals, non-whites, non-Christians and so forth. God's Way community particularly focused on Catholics, African-Americans, Jews, homosexuals, drug users, city dwellers, and liberals. This was partly based on a typology that Abraham had created in the early years of the community, based on his own experiences; and partly it drew on a wider typology, common among conservative Protestants, of those held responsible for the moral decline of the USA. God's Way community's members particularly railed against the Clinton administration which they saw as filled with 'queers, druggies and niggers' whose shared goal was to 'corrupt' the nation. God's Way shared a view common among Protestant fundamentalists that there was an axis of 'fallen' working together to deliberately destroy the nation by spreading their agenda (characterised as secular, liberal, amoral and relativistic) through all social institutions and throughout government. This leads to high levels of distrust of federal government and its agencies and the popularity of conspiracy theories among fundamentalists and other conservative Protestants. But in a sense the 'fallen' have a crucial role to play in the fundamentalist cosmos in that they are tasked with 'corrupting' and 'subverting' society and therefore help to facilitate the end of the world.

Most conservative Protestants have sufficient shared values to claim a loose kinship, despite the differences between evangelicals and fundamentalists. This kinship allows them to work together on political campaigns and typically means that different churches and communities categorise each other as 'chosen' or as 'true believers'. Some might even view other conservative Christians or even those of other religions as 'devout' and 'not fallen', but possibly misled. Although God's way community view themselves as uniquely 'chosen' by God, they do not view other Protestant fundamentalists or evangelicals as 'fallen'; instead they are seen as 'good people' who are 'trying to be chosen'. In other words they have the potential to achieve this status and perhaps join the community one day; their post-apocalyptic destiny was however still in question. The community's members enjoyed their relationships with neighbouring fundamentalist churches and friendships had been established, so they struggled with the contradiction that their neighbours were not 'chosen' but not 'fallen'. Discussion of how to categorise such 'good people' tended to fall quickly into silence in the face of potential doctrinal contradictions. The community did not view other believers, such as Jews, Muslims or Catholics, however devout or traditional, as 'true believers'. Liberal Christians were seen as especially 'fallen' as they 'pretended' to be devout while condoning Biblical Criticism, denying literalism and showing a high degree of tolerance on issues such as homosexuality and abortion. The 'fallen' were seen as making the 'Devil's work' easy for him and were viewed as the groups of people who would either willingly join the army of the Anti-Christ at Armageddon or who would be easily fooled by his promises during The Tribulation. The different categories of 'fallen' and the construction of a demonology of the 'fallen' will be explored in more depth in Chapter 7.

Chapter 5

The 'Right' Way: Orthodoxy and Orthopraxy in Everyday Life

The previous chapter explored the central aspect of God's Way community's identity: their belief in being 'chosen'. It was stressed that this belief means that the community view themselves as upholders of the 'true' orthodoxy and orthopraxy for Protestants (and indeed all Christians). It also means that the community set themselves strict behaviour codes for living, based on the view that their status as 'chosen' can be taken from them by God, at any time they appear to be not living up to, this status. This chapter will outline the key rules for living and believing within the community and will explore how everyday living itself is seen as an act of worship. It will also discuss the similarities in attitudes to moral issues, family life and gender roles between God's Way community and the wider community of American Protestant fundamentalists.

How the 'Chosen' should live: Orthodoxy and Orthopraxy

Fundamentalists of all religions consider themselves to be *the* upholders of the orthodoxy and orthopraxy of their particular faith and that everyone else is either following a wrong path or has deviated from the 'true' way (Barr, 1977, Marty and Appleby, 1991). Obviously, orthodoxy and orthopraxy emerge from a central belief in being 'chosen'. A group who assert a unique status and relationship with God inevitably need to view themselves as the 'true' believers, and therefore they become preoccupied with issues of orthodoxy and orthopraxy (Barr, 1977, Scott Jones, 2009). Such issues allow them to explore the nature of their status. Orthodoxy and orthopraxy allow groups to set themselves apart as 'different' and 'special' from other groups and also aid the reinforcement of a strong identity and worldview (Kanter, 1972, McGinn, 1994). Orthodoxy and orthopraxy are twin concepts; each feeds of the other. The notion of a core set of 'true' beliefs that are the 'right' beliefs do not make much sense, unless this establishes a 'true' or 'right ' way of living according to that belief system. Similarly, living in a style that you believe is the 'true' way lacks much sense unless attached to a wider belief framework that asserts that one conducts oneself according to these beliefs. Without one, you cannot have the other. God's Way community exhibit a range of orthodoxy and orthopraxy that is similar to that seen across American Protestant fundamentalism (Marsden, 1980, Ammerman, 1993, Carpenter, 1997).

God's Way community's central orthodoxy maintains a number of key beliefs that they see as 'true' beliefs. These include:

- They are the 'chosen' and are doing God's work.
- They have a God given role and destiny.
- The *Old Testament* and the *Books of Abraham* are the inerrant, literal words of God.
- There are absolute rights and wrongs in relation to all moral and social behaviour.
- They demonstrate their beliefs through everything that they do, not just through formal worship.
- The (secular) world external to the community is potentially 'polluting' and participation within it must be controlled to lessen its 'contaminating' influence.

This orthodoxy is reflected within the wider American Protestant fundamentalist community where moral absolutism and Biblical literalism are key tenets within a worldview that is predicated on a sense of 'special status' and destiny (Barr, 1977). The wider Protestant fundamentalist community also stress separatism in relation to the non-Protestant fundamentalist world. However, this community do tend to live physically in the secular world, while controlling its mental and spiritual influence via the establishment of their own parallel institutions, such as home schools, religious television channels and radio stations, colleges (for example, 'Liberty University'), publishing houses, record labels, and even theme parks (for example, *Heritage USA*), as well as participation in their own socio-spiritual networks. Strict monitoring within their communities also helps to alleviate external, secular influences that could be seen as 'dangerous'. This orthodoxy also establishes how communities should live and behave and again God's Way community's orthopraxy is similar in many ways to the wider Protestant fundamentalist community. However, as they particularly stress an emphasis on their perceived 'chosen' status, above all others who might be in their category, and as they have to maintain strict physical and social boundaries; orthopraxy becomes even more a central focus of daily living.

The Ritualisation of Everyday Life

Although God's Way community have a small chapel on their property; often several weeks can pass before they run a formal service of worship. Chapel services are often cancelled at the last minute if people are busy doing other tasks, particularly if it involves earning much needed income for the community. This at first may appear odd given that they profess to be the 'chosen' people of God; one might expect them to spend a great deal of time in their chapel in communal worship. However because they believe that their physical land is 'chosen' and that their community is 'chosen'; therefore all activity related to the maintaining and doing of everyday communal life, however trivial, becomes spiritually significant. Indeed all activity is seen as an 'act of worship'. Attendance at chapel services was not compulsory and often members saw the services as entertainment, through the communal singing of songs, rather than a form of serious worship. One member illustrated the communal view on this by saying 'God's around all the time, don't see no need to sit in no chapel when my back aches so'. She saw her daily participation in community life as sufficient to show her commitment to her faith. While another identified visible participation in worship as something associated with the 'fallen; 'they need to force folk into church, when true chosen have got God all the time'. In other words, those who are not 'true' believers have to place a great emphasis on visible, formal, participative worship to try to convince themselves and God that they are 'chosen'. However the community's view is that this 'showing off' in worship will ultimately fail to convince God because those who know that they are 'chosen' know that it is about what one does in one's everyday living, not just at a weekly, church service. Other Protestant fundamentalist groups would still stress the importance of communal, weekly or even daily worship, particularly because they are living within the secular world. Nevertheless, such groups would also see the need to live life in a particular way as a demonstration of commitment to faith (Ammerman, 1991). There are parallels here with the attitude to faith in Islam, where more emphasis is on how life is lived according to faith rather than on formalised, weekly attendance at worship (Gilsenan, 1990).

The community's everyday commitment to their beliefs can be seen in a range of tasks that at first seem mundane. One key thing that can be seen in the community is an emphasis on silence, it can at times be eerily silent; talk has to be related to the task at hand. Debate about beliefs or general talk is seen as 'fallen' behaviour: literalists do not need to debate beliefs, they need to just believe, while idle chatter is seen as 'dangerous' as it might lead to immorality, for example, the sexes engaging in idle chatter might lead to sexual experimentation. Idle chatter is also seen as time wasting; the 'chosen' have literally no time to waste, their own or God's. Thus, unless members have to discuss the task that they are involved in, they prefer to remain quiet rather than fill a silence with talk. However, there is an exception to this rule and that is in the widespread and repetitive use of short phrases that reiterate their worldview and are seen to encourage and motivate members in their everyday lives. The two key ones are 'God sees dust' and 'we are as significant as dust'.

The community has a number of tasks which members must do on a daily basis, such as chop wood, wash the supper dishes and light the stoves. Such repetitive acts are labelled 'chores' and are always executed, ritualistically, in exactly the same way and are always accompanied by the same stock phrase. For example, once supper is finished a range of 'chores' must be done by the women of the community: dusting the dining hall, sweeping the floor, and washing up and clearing away the dishes. Each woman has a set task to do and is always assisted by one of the uninitiated girls. The post-suppertime 'chores' begin with all the women repeating the phrase 'God sees dust' and as they go about their work all that can be heard is the repetition of this phrase. Anybody who seems to be slacking in their activity will find they soon fall under the focus of the others who will direct the phrase towards them, as if as a warning. The dining hall is always spotless, which makes the evening cleaning rituals seem compulsive; but the women always claim to see tiny specks of dust or the hints of stains and there is much over-dramatised flicking away of imaginary specks of dust just as everyone thinks the cleaning is done. The evening tasks are done in a hurried fashion as if being conducted against a clock, even though there is no set time limit for the accomplishment of any task. The thoroughness of the cleaning is typical of the members' strong work ethic and thorough approach to any communal task. All 'chores' had to be done with what was termed a 'willing heart', in other words individuals had to approach all tasks as if each was their favourite thing to do; the task had to be done thoroughly and without signs of reluctance or slacking. Having a 'willing heart' was about showing your commitment to the community but more importantly, it demonstrated the individual's commitment to submit to God's will at any time and for any purpose. Therefore, this attitude towards communal tasks was in itself an act of grace towards God. Members who exhibited a less than 'willing heart' received constant nagging and censure from everyone else, usually with stark reminders that the individual in question might jeopardise the entire community's future spiritual health.

The phrase 'God sees dust' originates from the longer phrase 'we are as significant as dust' which is in the *Books of Abraham*. The latter phrase has a clear meaning; it is a reminder that even though the community are 'the chosen' they must not rise above their station and become 'full' of themselves. The phrase reminds them that their significance is small in the divine grand scheme of things; it is an expression of humility. The shorter 'God sees dust' has a twofold meaning when said during 'chores'; firstly, it reminds the community that God can see everything and therefore anything that detracts from their 'chosen' status (even 'dust') will be seen. In other words, God does not miss a thing. Secondly, the phrase reminds the community that God sees them (whom he views as 'dust') and is always watching. Casting themselves, symbolically, as 'dust' also reiterates their precarious relationship with God; he could literally wipe them away as one would wipe away dust from a bookcase. The repetitive use of 'God sees dust' during all kinds of 'chores' around the community allows the members to express and reinforce their worldview through everyday activity. 'We are as significant as dust' was often repeated during tasks that were deemed less pleasant, such as, the external farm labouring that many of the members did to generate much needed income for the community or during the cleaning out of the pens of the community's animals. The phrase featured prominently during the women's quilting and embroidery sessions and was sewn into quilts, cushions and pillows.

During mealtimes, where most of the food consumed has been grown on their land, the members will highly praise the food, with sayings like 'God himself gave us these beans' or 'God would drink this water it's so pure'. This highly ritualised way of conducting communal tasks expresses their commitment to belief and reiterates their worldview through everyday activity; activity that has to be done in the 'correct' set way every time. As the communal space, physical and mental is 'chosen', all tasks that are related to its maintenance therefore become symbolically and literally, acts of worship with greater significance than any chapel service might have. Communal activities also reflect other aspects of their belief system.

Views of Gender

Most communal tasks express a strict gender division of labour that is justified through their literal reading of scripture. God Way community, in common with most other Protestant fundamentalists, view the Biblical account, in the *Book of Genesis*, of Adam and Eve as literal and the basis for all gender roles and responsibilities (Ammerman, 1993, Bendroth, 1994). How men and women should be and how they should act is therefore divinely proscribed, fixed and inerrant. Men, like Adam, are seen to have been created in God's image to lead and rule over all other things, including women and children. In Protestant fundamentalism, generally, men are therefore seen as spiritual leaders because they are deemed to be closer to God and are tasked as instrumental and spiritual providers, protectors and leaders of their families and communities (Ammerman, 1993, Bendroth, 1994). As well as the figure of Adam, other Biblical figures are invoked to account for this male role, for example, Moses. In addition, God's Way community use the figure of their founder Abraham as an exemplar of masculinity. Fundamentalists, typically, stress traditional, western, hegemonic masculinity as the norm: heterosexual, strong, assertive, knowing, unemotional and powerful (Connell, 1995). The men of God's Way community are no different in this regard: they see their job as to provide and protect their women and children, while also offering spiritual leadership. Although the community have a leader in Isaac Zion, communal decision making lies with the regular meetings of the community's married men. Thus, communal and spiritual power lies with men and for a woman to seek participation in the men's meetings would be deemed 'unfeminine' and going against God's gender order. The granting in secular society of political rights to women, as well as legislation that allows women to work and be treated as equal to men, were seen by the community's members as 'wrong' and 'evil' because it went against the divine order of things. The wider Protestant fundamentalist community have been campaigning against any ERA legislation since the 1970s and are vocal opponents of all measures to encourage women, especially mothers, into the world of work (Ammerman, 1991, Carpenter, 1997). The community's view of masculine power is linked to marriage and fatherhood; both bring with it 'full' adult status, thus, unmarried men had no place in the decision making process of the community. The association of marriage and fatherhood with status and power is common in a range of cultures past and present, but it does place pressure on single men to find a suitable marriage partner (Connell, 2002).

As with masculinity, fundamentalists also stress a traditional hegemonic view of femininity that is also based on scripture: women are subordinate to men generally and their husbands specifically (Connell, 2002, Ammerman, 1993, Bendroth, 1994). The figure of Eve, who was made from Adam and thus is not cast in God's image but is a secondary figure in the Creation story, is the basis for this view of the female role. Women's destiny is to marry and be mothers. The central focus of a woman's life is to be other-oriented; putting her needs last behind those of her husband, her children and her community. Women are seen as emotional, physically fragile and in need of protection from men; endless scriptural references reinforce this viewpoint. The symbolic figure of Eve reminds both men and women that the latter were responsible for the Fall of mankind. The story of Eve also reiterates the view that knowledge is not safe in the hands of women and that women cannot be trusted fully to keep God's word, in other words, they need men to take control. The community's women were not weak or submissive individuals, but rather saw it as an act of spiritual and emotional strength to allow themselves to be subordinate to their husbands and fathers. A woman acting in a dominant or 'masculine' way was seen as something 'unnatural' but also this was seen as 'too easy' a role for women to play; submerging your needs and desires into looking after everyone else was seen as a much harder role to play. The older women of the community regularly reiterated the view that life was 'hard but God knows his women are strong'. Both men and women acknowledged that a woman who lacked a strong father or husband was prone to become overbearing which was dangerous for her (physically, mentally and spiritually) as she was not 'built' for such a role; but also bad for society at large. Many of the ills of contemporary society, such as, the seemingly high rates of divorce, illegitimacy, delinquency and homosexuality, were seen as a result of men and women transgressing their traditional, Biblically ordained roles. This view again is expressed more widely in the Protestant fundamentalist community at large (LaHaye, 1980). For example, the high divorce rate was seen by the community's members as a consequence of women acting like men; no wonder the marriages failed, what husband wants a strong wife was their view. However, the moral decline of secular society was not just blamed on women trying to 'be men' but also on men failing to act 'like men should': men abandoning their role as fathers and refusing to take leadership roles, were also seen to have encouraged the rise of 'immorality'. The perception of a crisis in masculinity within society has led to a number of masculinity movements in Protestant fundamentalism that has attracted participants from across the conservative Christian population. For example, the 'Promise Keepers', seek to encourage men to become 'godly influences' in their families, communities and nation, with seven pledges to be 'better men' (www.promisekeepers.org) and the 'Men of Integrity' stress 'spiritual muscle' for men to 'serve' their families and be a 'godly example to your wife and children' (www.menofintegrity.org). These organisations seek to encourage men to embrace traditional masculine roles and to not shy away from being strong (and spiritual) husbands and fathers. They organise camp meetings, conferences and via their websites offer a range of educational books and DVDs. Their vision of masculinity (and indeed femininity) draws heavily on scriptural accounts. Such groups consider many current social problems to be caused by the decline in traditional masculinity.

The community's women saw great fulfilment in their roles as wives and mothers; they did not understand why women in the secular world would wish to work or remain unmarried. This view of femininity is typical across Protestant fundamentalism (Ammerman, 1993, Bendroth, 1994) and even spilled over into the brief secular trend of the 'Surrendered Wives' guide to successful marriage that was a media sensation in the early Noughties. The book (Doyle, 1999) played into long standing media and cultural stereotypes of the working mother and the consequences for children, families and society generally. The book suggested that contemporary women were unhappy trying to play so many 'unfeminine' roles and suggested that true happiness would come with women following the model of fundamentalist women by 'surrendering' to their husbands and families and subsuming themselves within the domestic sphere. Although the 'surrendered wives' movement still operates; its long-term success is questionable as it offers a secularised version of what fundamentalist women see as an act of faith; without the attachment to a wider belief system (and a faith in that system) it is doomed to fail as a self-help guide. The community's women stressed the importance in 'men being men' and found trends like 'house husbands', 'mannies' and men being emotional as funny and also 'unnatural'. The transgression of gender roles was seen as going against the divine order of things and its consequence could be seen in the decline in moral values, marriage and the growth of a range of social problems, such as crime and drug abuse.

A sense of modesty for both sexes was reinforced through the community's dress code which stressed that both sexes 'cover up' and avoided showing any flesh below the neck except forearms. Even on hot days the men would remain shirted. The actual clothes worn by members were quite unisex; overalls, baggy jeans, plaid shirts, and leather work boots were standard. On special occasions the women would wear long dresses that covered legs and only showed a glimpse of ankle. Tight clothing was prohibited and bathing suits were only allowed in single sex swimming. This modesty had to be maintained despite a communal architecture that facilitated surveillance. Everyone dressed and changed in the bathroom, and long and baggy night attire aided nocturnal modesty. Modesty was seen as reinforcing gender roles, particularly for women, but more importantly was seen as a means to reduce sexual desire, curiosity or immorality, particularly among the community's unmarried adults and teenagers. A similar concern with modesty in terms of dress can be seen across conservative Protestantism in the USA; although without the strict code of God's Way community. The recent furore over the stage costumes of Miley Cyrus or a decade ago, the outfits of Britney Spears (both singers from conservative Protestant backgrounds with a mass appeal), illustrates this concern particularly in relation to children and teenagers.

Views of Sexuality

Sexuality and sexual behaviour, like gender, are understood through recourse to
scripture and are linked to gender roles. The community again follow the pattern
of wider Protestant fundamentalism by stressing that sexuality is God given and
that monogamous heterosexuality is the only 'normal' sexuality. Numerous *Old
Testament* passages, particularly the *Book of Leviticus*, are used to justify this
heteronormative model. Sexuality is seen as a 'gift' from God in order to have
children; thus for God's Way community sex is seen purely as a reproductive act
and not as an activity that might also be enjoyed in a recreational sense. Sex is
also something that can only occur within marriage where it can be controlled and
regulated, again as recommended by Biblical scripture (Ammerman, 1993).

Christianity has always problematised sex and sexuality more so than Judaism
and Islam (Wiesner, 2000). The founding myth of all three faiths is the story of
Adam and Eve in the *Book of Genesis*; in that story, God punishes mankind forever
with the concept of 'original sin' for Adam and Eve's failure to obey God. The
story also associates bodily awareness with shame (Weeks, 1989). The 'solution'
in Judaism and Islam is marriage, that can regulate sexual desire and activity;
and direct it towards reproduction. Sex within marriage, in either faith, is seen as
unproblematic and indeed both religions stress the important role sexual pleasure
can play in maintaining a happy relationship. Christianity's focus on the figure
of Jesus who is the product of a Virgin Birth further problematises sexuality,
particularly female sexuality. The veneration of the Madonna who is able to have
a baby without sin (i.e. through sex) places an impossible ideal upon ordinary
Christian women who are not able to reproduce without sinning. In addition, the
story of Jesus, especially his Resurrection is concerned with rising above bodily
frailties and stressing spiritual strength. Thus Christianity in particular has a
problem with the body generally and sexuality specifically (Wiesner, 2000). The
early Christians stressed celibacy but soon had to compromise and accept sex
within marriage. In Christianity, sex was only for procreation, within marriage;
and celibacy was viewed as the ideal. In Mediaeval Europe, there was a complex
list of rules concerning when married couples could and could not have sex, for
example, sex was forbidden on Sundays, Saints days or when the woman was
pregnant (Wiesner, 2000). These attitudes towards sex and sexuality profoundly
influenced western norms and values until the latter half of the twentieth century
(Weeks, 1989). Liberal and mainstream Christianity today still tends to stress the
importance of monogamy and marriage while increasingly moving away from
strict moral proscriptions. Protestant fundamentalists maintain the historical
Christian view that sex is 'dangerous' for the soul and must be controlled through
monogamous, heterosexual marriage that stresses its reproductive role. Within
that view, there is variation as to the role sex may play within marriage beyond a
reproductive function (see for example, LaHaye and LaHaye, 1998); God's Way
community take an absolute line that sex is only for reproduction. This contention
is linked to the idea of purity; if one is 'chosen' then what one does with one's body

can affect its 'purity' levels. Premarital sex, homosexual sex, oral sex and sex 'just' for pleasure is seen as spiritually 'impure'; and physically and spiritually damaging due to the fact that the Bible makes it very clear how such sexual acts should be viewed. However, more mainstream Protestant fundamentalism acknowledges the importance of sex not just for reproduction but also for the maintenance of a healthy marital relationship. Thus abstinence movements are not against sex per se but against it outside of marriage (see for example, True Life Waits at www. lifeway.com/tlw). Sex, sexuality and related issues were not discussed openly in God's Way community except in relation to the condemnation of homosexuality and the importance of chastity and marriage. Reproductive-related processes, such as menstruation and menopause, were only discussed in single sex groups, and even then in hushed, slightly embarrassed tones.

God's Way community, as with most mainstream Protestant fundamentalism stress premarital chastity and are against any form of sex education as it is seen as encouraging immoral activity. God's Way's teenagers were taught at their fundamentalist school about chastity and the importance of abstinence; that was their sex education. They had all joined the True Love Waits (www.lifeway.com/ tlw) abstinence movement and had pledged to refrain from any sexual activity until they married. True Love Waits is one of a number of abstinence movements, another one being the Silver Ring Thing (www.silverringthing.com), popular in the USA among fundamentalist and conservative Protestants where teenagers pledge to refrain from sex until marriage. With True Love Waits they sign and then carry a 'pledge' card to show their abstinence, whereas with the Silver Ring Thing teenagers wear a special silver ring to show their commitment to their pledge. The Bush administration offered vocal support to such movements and ten states have abstinence-only sex education in schools. God's Way community are also against contraception partly because they see it as encouraging sexual promiscuity and sex for pleasure, rather than for procreation. The community's teenagers are taught that contraception is 'evil' not just, because it interferes with God's 'natural' plan but also because it encourages physical desires that can 'pollute' the soul. They stress that condoms might prevent sexually transmitted diseases but that they cannot stop the spread of 'sin' that will 'infect' the soul.

Homosexuality was viewed by God's Way community as 'unnatural' and against God's plan for both gender and sex because it encouraged, in their view, men to act like women and women to act like men. It also is seen as encouraging sex for pleasure only (thus breaking the important link between sex and reproduction) as such unions cannot, naturally, produce children. Again, scripture, such as the *Book of Leviticus*, was quoted to justify this view. This view of homosexuality again shows God's Way's connectedness to the wider Protestant fundamentalist community who tend to view homosexuality as 'unnatural, 'sinful' and symptomatic of a psychological disease (see for example, Homosexuals Anonymous, www.ha-fs.org). A popular fundamentalist slogan often shouted at gay rights campaigners is 'Adam and Eve, not Adam and Steve' to illustrate the view that God created two sexes for a very specific purpose and homosexuality is wrong because it 'transgresses that divine order. God's Way community believed that all homosexuals should be 'killed' and that homosexuality was rife at the heart of government; they believed that President Clinton and his wife were 'homos' who spread sexual immorality throughout the federal government. They viewed the increasing visibility of homosexuals in the media and elsewhere as a 'sign' that the end of the world was coming. They also identified AIDs as a 'God given' disease which was sent to 'wipe out' homosexuals and other sexual 'criminals'. Again, this has been a commonly held view amongst Protestant fundamentalists (as well as other types of conservative Christians) since the emergence of AIDs in the early 1980s. Protestant fundamentalists, including God's Way community, view homosexuality as a 'choice' that individuals make due to traumatic events in childhood such as sexual abuse or because parents have failed to offer positive gender roles. In other words, one is not born gay but is 'made' gay. However, the community do not believe that there is any point in 'treating' homosexuals or encouraging them to change, as they view them as similar to drug addicts and paedophiles: they are unable to lose their addictions. They therefore had no time for the 'curing sexual brokeness' movements that are common in protestant fundamentalist communities. Organisations like Exodus International, National Association for Research and Therapy of Homosexuality (NARTH) and Homosexuals Anonymous offer 'treatment' for homosexuality and ultimately 'cures' through a rejection of the 'homosexual lifestyle choice', counselling to locate the 'cause' of the 'sexual broken-ness', and intense Biblical study. Celibacy or marriage are seen as possible means to 'cure' so-called 'sexual brokeness'. Homosexuals Anonymous apes the twelve step program popularised by Alcoholics Anonymous, through offering a fourteen step program to 'cure' 'sexual brokeness'. These controversial organisations particularly target teenagers' burgeoning sexuality, and feed into a wider fundamentalist view that all forms of 'sexual immorality' are destroying the moral fabric of the nation. This view of sexuality has little basis in mainstream scientific or psychological thinking and such 'treatment' programs have been heavily criticised by associations like the American Psychiatric Association. It has also been well parodied in the media, for example in the film *But I'm a Cheerleader*, released in 1999.

Protestant fundamentalists view homosexuality, sexual promiscuity, premarital sexual activity and sex education in schools, as encouraging the moral decline of society (LaHaye and LaHaye, 1998). 'Sexual immorality' is also identified as a key cause of a range of social problems, such as the high national rates of teenage pregnancy, youth delinquency, divorce, illiteracy, sexually transmitted diseases, child abuse, rape and drug addiction. Because Protestant fundamentalists' view themselves as 'keepers' of the national soul it means that moral issues become particularly significant in their battle to 'save' America and uphold its status as a 'chosen' nation. This is one of the central reasons why campaigning on moral issues has been a key strategy of Protestant fundamentalism since the 1950s. Chapter 8 will explore moral campaigning in more detail.

Children

God's Way community view children as a 'gift' from God and because of that are against contraception and abortion, which they see as 'murder'. Again, such views are common across protestant fundamentalism and why fundamentalist sex education programs focus on abstinence over contraception; it is also why anti-abortion campaigns (such as 'Operation Rescue') have been a central tenet of fundamentalist campaigning since *Roe v. Wade* in 1973. Children are viewed by God's Way community as not quite fully 'chosen'; they are vulnerable, physically, emotionally and spiritually because of this. Therefore, children have to be protected from all potentially damaging influences that might damage their potential as future 'chosen' and lead them astray. That means that the community's adults see it as a joint responsibility to discipline and guide children. The community use corporal punishment on a regular basis on children of all ages and see 'tough love' as emulating the sort of love that God himself gives out. Studies (see for example, Ellinson, 1996) have shown that Protestant fundamentalists generally show higher than expected levels of corporal punishment in their communities. There is certainly a discourse of 'spare the rod, spoil the child'. Protestant fundamentalist communities place great emphasis on the monitoring of children, both within their communities and in relation to external influences upon them. The emergence of Christian rock and rap music is one example of a response to a secular 'threat' to fundamentalist youth. Similarly, most communities have youth groups, churches and summer camps; the infamous documentary *Jesus Camp*, released in 2006, illustrates the sorts of activities and ethos common in such summer camps. God's Way community send their teenagers to a Christian Bible summer camp and only allow them to watch Christian television channels or pre-screened family style films. Even then, there is constant vigilance concerning content, for example, while I was living in the community a communal viewing of *The Sound of Music* was interrupted, as the video was fast forwarded through a scene where an unmarried couple kissed. The scene was not considered appropriate viewing for children or teenagers as it went against the community's teaching on premarital chastity, which included no romantic kissing outside of marriage. A similar example was during a trip to a local supermarket to buy some ice cream. The group of teenagers had been picked up from their local Christian school and while we waited near the checkout, some of the adults quickly ushered us all out of the store. The reason had been that a magazine stand near where we stood had featured a fashion magazine with a model showing a bare midriff; this was deemed too 'pornographic' for the teenagers to see. A similar vigilance can be seen in the wider Protestant fundamentalist community in campaigns against nudity, sex, bad language, and so forth in the media, particularly related to children's entertainment (Ammerman, 1993).

The Importance of Family

Family life was viewed by God's Way community as important for the stability of young adults, providing them with a source of identity and responsibility. Because of the community's small population, a growing group of single men and women were emerging who would be unable to marry within the group due to existing kinship ties. The dearth of new members meant that the long-term prospects for their respective marriages looked gloomy. These singles were stigmatised as 'silly', 'lazy' and always looking for 'mischief'; even if these labels did not reflect reality. Being adult and single was seen as a tainted status, which went against God's plan; the growing national trend of 'childless by choice' couples, as well as the rising numbers of single men and women was seen as 'unnatural' and further damaging to the 'soul' of the nation.

As has been mentioned before 'full' adult status on the community was gained through marriage and parenthood; for men this gave them the right to influence communal decisions and for women it brought status in the division of domestic 'chores'. Single status members, although initiated adults, were always viewed as 'lesser' to the married members. Infertility was also problematic as it raised questions about moral character; one of the older married women ('Martha') had been unable to have children and was viewed as having 'done something' in her past (she had joined the community in her twenties) before she had married. Her infertility was seen as proof that God punishes the 'chosen' even more seriously than he punishes the 'fallen' as he expects better of the 'chosen'. The woman in question agreed with this view of her status and saw it as proof that God 'missed nothing' and 'expected much'. She tended to avoid too much contact with the community's young children (for fear of 'damaging' them) and took on 'chores' that could be accomplished alone or in a small group in order to minimise what she saw as her 'dirty influence'. No question mark was placed over her husband's moral character or past life; his wife carried their burden of infertility alone. This view of infertility is still commonplace in Protestant fundamentalism and such couples would not have recourse to fertility treatment as such treatment is seen as humans trying to do 'God's work'. The donation of sperm or eggs that might be involved in such treatments would also not be an option for individuals who consider themselves 'special' or 'chosen' as the spiritual status of the donors would be hard to ascertain.

Self and Communal Monitoring

Communities that stress strict behaviour codes, for moral and other reasons, rely on systems of monitoring to ensure compliance; otherwise, rules might break down over time, particularly in the face of external influences. Communal monitoring must be sufficient to encourage conformity but not so totalising as to appear oppressive (Kanter, 1972, Hechter, 1987). Groups, like God's Way community, who live in intentional communities that are separated, physically and/or socially, from the rest of society, can monitor behaviour in subtle ways through the act of everyday communal living; one cannot literally escape the 'gaze' of other members. The absence of doors within God's Way's communal spaces further facilitates this monitoring process as conversations can be listened to and activities literally observed. The listening and watching of others was openly done and accepted as a normal part of everyday life, as illustrated by older members shouting through doorways to, typically, younger members who might be doing little work and chatting; reminding them that 'God sees dust'. The communal houses were all heated via central wood burning stoves that distributed heat throughout the dwellings via floor vents. These vents had the side-effect of transmitting noises from one room to another, meaning that it was relatively easy to eavesdrop on conversations in other parts of the house. Again it was seen as acceptable behaviour to acknowledge that you had been eavesdropping if it meant that any 'deviant' behaviour or attitudes were thwarted. However, members found ways to participate in private conversations through working with individuals that they knew shared their views and with whom they felt safe discussing non-orthodox views. These sorts of conversations usually occurred off-community, while on shopping trips, school pick-ups, or during farm labouring trips; all of which were less monitored.

Individual members of the community who seem to be shirking from their 'chores' or showing anything less than a 'willing heart', as mentioned previously, are soon the focus of chastisement from others in the group. A good example of this was the ongoing stigmatisation of Eve, Isaac's eldest daughter, who was notoriously slow at chores and used her almost constant state of pregnancy as a reason to shirk work. She was seen as having an 'unwilling heart' and faced constant nagging and vilification from the older women in particular. Eve was used as an example for the children and teenagers of how not to behave and members worried constantly for her 'soul'. There was also widespread concern that Eve's behaviour would not only encourage others to follow her lead, but that the very 'chosen' status of the entire community might be ultimately jeopardised. Thus, those like Eve, who deviated from the community's work ethic or general ethos not only placed their own future at risk but ultimately that of the whole community. This led to a culture where it was normal for members to inform the others of any behaviour deemed 'fallen' that they had witnessed. Even the children had absorbed this message as demonstrated one day when a couple of the teenage boys had sneaked a magazine that they had picked up at school from another student, onto the community. The magazine was a harmless cars and trucks title but it did feature scantily clad female models. The magazine remained hidden for several days until one of the youngest children (Leah) informed Isaac of its presence. The child, who was seven, did this saying 'what if tomorrow's judgement day'; in other words if the end of the world was literally about to happen, this 'forbidden' magazine's presence on the community might jeopardise all of their futures. Isaac's response to the magazine incident was to burn the offending title in front of the whole community and to beat the boys in question with his belt, again in front of the entire community. Deviance is therefore minimised, and via this monitoring, conformity is reinforced.

Older members actively monitor and censor external influences, thus eliminating a wide range of potentially disruptive sources. For example, they decide what radio or television stations are appropriate and are poised to switch off anything that is seen as 'corrupting'. Similarly, newspapers, books and magazines are vetted. The children and teenagers are rarely left without adult supervision; their attendance at school being the only time that they are away from the 'gaze' of the community's adults. In the wider fundamentalist community, monitoring is also prevalent, particularly in relation to children and adolescents. As most fundamentalists live in the secular world, rather than on intentional communities, the role of monitors falls to parents, teachers and pastors. There is also a greater emphasis on censoring potentially damaging 'external' influences and promoting fundamentalist alternatives, for example, Christian television, rap and rock music, summer camps, and theme parks.

Similarly, groups need individuals to internalise rules of behaviour and in effect self-regulate (Kanter, 1972, Hechter, 1987). Self-regulation is easier to develop and maintain in religious communities because of the legitimising power of such beliefs. The behaviour of Martha and Leah discussed previously both demonstrate the degree to which the community's members, old and young alike, have internalised its belief system. The belief in both an individual and communal 'chosen' identity and therefore relationship to God, ensures that the majority of members show a high degree of commitment to self-regulation. Indeed, in private, individuals, particularly the women, would agonise over whether their behaviour was 'good enough' and would chastise themselves over seemingly minor lapses of commitment, such as, sighing and 'feeling weary' before a task. The struggle to maintain appropriate levels of religiosity and commitment, has always been a component of Protestantism generally, and fundamentalism in particular (Ammerman, 1993). To admit that faith is a struggle is seen as a sign of humility and demonstrates that faith and one's relationship with God is not fixed, but a constant evolution. The role of personal testimony of faith (and the struggle in maintaining faith) has always been a key component of revivals, Bible conferences and other gatherings of conservative Protestants (Marsden, 1980). Such testimonies are seen as a means to rally the faithful and encourage the idea that faith, even for those deemed closest to God, is always a challenge. They remain a fixture of Christian broadcasting (Harding, 2000). Giving testimony is a means to process the demands of self-regulation and helps to reinforce communal norms. God's Way community participated in communal testimony-giving, which was seen as a means to inspire the younger members; the group also participated in local fundamentalist gatherings where they would give and receive testimony, something which most found inspiring and cathartic.

The high degree of focus on orthodoxy and orthopraxy among fundamentalists allows them to demonstrate and outline their identity as 'chosen', as well as a means to actively live-out their worldview. It also links their everyday behaviour to their ultimate destiny: to survive the end of the world and live on Earth by God's side.

Chapter 6
'Counting Down the Days': Apocalyptic Urgency and Agency

Protestant fundamentalists believe themselves to be specially 'chosen' by God and this leads them, as the last chapter illustrated, to stress orthodoxy and orthopraxy in their everyday lives. However, this belief in a special status and the zeal for strict monitoring and regulation of behaviour and belief, is meaningless unless tied to an apocalyptic vision. In other words, there is no point in identifying as 'chosen' and choosing to live a particular way unless that activity and belief has direction. A belief that the world will end, and at that ending the 'chosen' will be 'saved' is the ultimate validation of the fundamentalist worldview; without it, there is a lack of meaning, direction and purpose. The identity of 'being chosen' needs an ultimate destiny; otherwise, what makes the 'chosen' any different from other so-called believers or indeed non-believers? Apocalypticism is therefore a key aspect of the fundamentalist worldview. For fundamentalists, apocalypticism not only gives meaning and reinforcement to their worldview (and identity) but is also a useful tool in their political campaigning.

What is Apocalypticism?

All cultures, past and present, have eschatological beliefs, that are beliefs in an end to the world; similarly, all cultures have beliefs concerning creation. In a sense, you cannot have one set of beliefs without the other; beginnings only make sense if there are also endings. Myths about endings are powerful because they tap into our fear of death and the related (and perhaps ultimate) existential question: 'is there life after death'. Weber (1991) makes the point that most individuals and cultures prefer to live in a meaningful universe; thus, we impose meaning upon the world. Eschatological beliefs serve an essential role in giving meaning not just to beginnings and endings, but also in explaining everyday existence. In our increasingly secularised world, long-standing religious accounts of creation (for example, Chapter One of the *Book of Genesis*) have been seriously challenged by scientific discoveries; but such scientific accounts fail to fully provide a meaningful (at a human level) account of what happens when the world ends or indeed explain the point of existence generally. The 'Big Crunch' may be a scientifically accurate account of the universe's predicted demise but it lacks meaning at the level of human significance. Similarly, few take comfort in the view that on their death, biological decay will eventually return them to the earth; most people still seek to cling on to the notion of an afterlife in which they still have agency and more importantly significance (Bruce, 2002, Davie, 1994, Davie, 2002). The recurring use of end of the world imagery in popular culture (Boyer, 1992), particularly in films, for example, *The Day after Tomorrow* (2004) and *2012* (2009), shows the continuing appeal of eschatological imagery.

Most eschatological beliefs revolve around the idea that at some future date, cataclysmic change will occur and a new order will be established. In ancient cultures, such as the Aztecs, Greeks, and Babylonians, there was a view that the ending signified a righting of the cosmic order that had been decaying since its creation (Eliade 1963: 54–74). Such cultures tended to be polytheistic and have a cyclic view of cosmic time; that is, birth, growth, decay, destruction, are in a constant cycle directed by the actions and interactions of Gods and mortals. The cycle is 'rebooted' following the end-time events. In such systems, the Gods judge cultures, as opposed to individuals. However, in monotheistic faiths we see a different type of eschatological belief, which can be classed as 'apocalyptic'.

The word 'apocalypse' is Greek in origin and means 'revelation' or 'unveiling'. Apocalyptic beliefs relate specifically to beliefs, which give 'details of the future course of history and the imminence of its divinely appointed end' (McGinn 1979: 3). In other words, whereas eschatological beliefs, generally, predict an end to the world, they are vague as to when or why that might occur. Apocalypticism is a belief that the date of the end of the world is already set by God and will be revealed via 'signs' that 'true' believers will be able to interpret. Typically such 'signs' can be found within scriptural sources, like the Bible or Koran. Thus, apocalypticism is a subset of eschatological beliefs.

Apocalyptic beliefs predominate in monotheistic religions (Burkitt, 1914, McGinn, 1994), such as Judaism, Christianity and Islam, because the switch to monotheism involves two key changes within a belief system. First of all the adoption of a belief in one God, as opposed to many, represents an abstraction in which God becomes all powerful and encompassing (Berger, 1967). God shifts from being human-like to being distant, all knowing but also inscrutable. This means that believers must place greater importance on orthodoxy and orthopraxy as a means to please God and in order to gauge God's reaction. In polytheistic systems, one can approach a specific God with a specific issue and as long as that God is kept happy, then the consequences of human behaviour can be controlled. In addition, polytheistic systems have a typically cyclical view of cosmic time, whereas monotheistic systems adopt a linear view of time. Such a view of time, with a belief in a distinct beginning, middle and ending, is predicated on 'something' happening at each distinct stage, especially the beginning and ending. The beginning and ending give meaning to each other, without one, the other is meaningless. The development of a belief in one God encourages beliefs in being 'special' or 'chosen'; that is, God is 'our' God and has a relationship with us as 'true' believers in contrast to those who do not believe in 'our' God. This can be seen in the development of monotheism in Judaism (Burkitt, 1914). A belief in being 'chosen' works best within a linear view of cosmic time, as the beginning and ending, events shape and reinforce this belief: why be 'chosen' unless this status results in a reward at the end that contrasts with a 'punishment' for those who are not 'chosen'. Thus, God creates the world in a particular way and demands that people act and believe in a specific manner. However, this creation makes no sense unless there is an ending where the ultimate purpose of creation will be revealed; after all, there is no point in believing or living a particular way unless there is an ultimate goal. Creation also establishes and constructs the concepts of good, evil and sin; thus, it feeds into orthodoxy and orthopraxy, and helps create the ultimate conflict between those who are 'chosen' and those who are 'fallen'. This 'othering' is essential for the maintenance of a 'chosen' worldview, which is discussed in greater detail in Chapter 7. Apocalyptic beliefs, like eschatological beliefs in general, focus on moral decay and the battle between the forces of 'good' and 'evil'; but in apocalyptic beliefs, God judges each individual in turn and decides each person's ultimate fate (McGinn, 1994). This places tremendous agency and pressure on the individual believer and means that religious communities must ensure that they have structures in place that facilitate and reinforce orthodoxy and orthopraxy, as outlined in the previous chapter.

Apocalypticism and Christianity

Christian apocalypticism builds on the earlier Judaic vision of the end of the world. In Judaism there is a belief in a final judgement, where God will 'save' the 'righteous' and the 'fallen' will perish. This belief fed into the Jewish view of predestination. However, mainstream Judaism has always stressed a focus on everyday living and believing as opposed to apocalyptic concerns. Christianity, on the other hand, was founded as an apocalyptic faith (McGinn 1994:2); as it is predicted on the belief that Jesus is the Messiah, whose coming was prophesised in the *Old Testament*. The life of Jesus establishes his messiah-like credentials; he is the product of a Virgin Birth, he can perform miracles and heal the sick, and is resurrected after death. However, acceptance of the belief that Jesus is the Messiah means acceptance of the belief that Jesus will return (the 'Second Coming') to lead the forces of 'good' against 'evil'. This role is outlined in the appropriately placed, final book of the *New Testament*, the *Book of Revelation*. Early Christianity was profoundly millennialist, with a belief that Jesus could return to Earth at any time (McGinn, 1979). This early version of apocalypticism was pre-millennialist in that the early Christians believed that Jesus would literally return to Earth before the Millennium, where he would reign for a thousand years before the 'Last Judgement' took place. Roman persecution of the early Christians amplified this apocalyptic belief; Christians interpreted their persecution as a sign that the 'Tribulation' had started. Thus, the early Christian apocalyptic vision is what is now labelled Post-Tribulation, Pre-millennialism (McGinn, 1979, 1994).

The 'Tribulation' is foretold in the *Gospel of St Matthew* (St Matthew 24: 29) as a period where the forces of evil, led by the Anti-Christ, gain control of the world and persecute the faithful. This period is characterised by moral and spiritual decline and culminates in the return of Jesus to lead the faithful in the final battle (often referred to as 'Armageddon') between the forces of 'good' and 'evil', which ends with victory for the 'faithful'. The *Book of Revelation*, which remains the key apocalyptic source for fundamentalist Protestants today, was written during this time of the Roman persecution of Christians. The writer, 'John', draws on the existing Jewish genre of apocalyptic writing to address his audience. The book urges them to keep the faith in the face of suffering and promises that an end is in sight, where the 'unfaithful' will be punished and the 'true' believers will be rewarded. The text also outlines the details of events that will culminate in this apocalypse. The *Book of Revelation* was written with a particular audience in mind and used symbolism and imagery that they would understand, in a sense it was a piece of religious propaganda to rally the troops and reinforce faith (McGinn, 1994). The text is read as literal by fundamentalists today, although it was written with a very different audience in mind, which means that the symbolism must be interpreted and made to fit contemporary events.

As the Christian church became established and powerful, it downplayed the belief in an imminent apocalypse and return of Jesus. The Council of Nicaea in 325 AD saw the codification of Christian doctrine, ritual and scripture; the *Book of Revelation* was almost omitted from the final accepted 'version' of the Bible, demonstrating that as Christianity became mainstream it began to downplay its apocalypticism. The Council of Ephesus in 431AD adopted the Augustinian view that the church should focus on everyday living and believing; and condemn millennialism. Millennialism encourages believers to focus on the future and see the present as insignificant and transient. St Augustine and the early Church leaders recognised that such an ethos would not build a strong and permanent church (McGinn, 1994). St Augustine also suggested that Biblical apocalyptic texts, such as the *Books of Daniel* and *Revelation* be taken allegorically rather than literally. The mainstream Christian view of predestination stressed that one could be 'saved' by following Church rules, rituals and doctrine. Predestination became tied to conformity to Church dogma. Increasingly individuals or groups that held on to apocalyptic beliefs were deemed 'heretical' and increasingly, suppressed (McGinn, 1979).

Apocalypticism and Protestantism

The Protestant Reformation that started in 1517 involved a number of changes to long-standing beliefs, particularly it sought to strip away church hierarchies and focus on the agency of the individual believer. In relation to apocalypticism, the Reformation saw an alteration in the belief in predestination. Protestantism embraced the idea that God had already 'chosen' everyone's destiny and that individuals were 'saved' or 'doomed' even before birth. How Protestants implemented this much starker and more absolute version of predestination varied across sects; however it gave rise to the view that God is ever vigilant and that individual conduct in everyday life impacts on one's spiritual 'health' and destiny. Thus, Protestantism is much more preoccupied with the monitoring of everyday living and believing (Lindberg, 2005). Catholicism stresses conformity to church ritual and practice, by receiving Communion, confessing sins and doing penance, one can maintain spiritual 'health'. Protestantism abandoned such rituals and required individuals (and groups) to take personal responsibility for their 'spiritual' health; we can see this attitude surviving in contemporary varieties of conservative Protestantism, particularly fundamentalism. However, the mainstream European Protestant churches shared the pre-existing Augustinian consensus on apocalypticism. Apocalypticism was an important aspect of belief for German Anabaptist and Pietist groups, but these groups were considered marginal within mainstream European Protestantism (McGinn, 1979, 1994).

By the eighteenth century, Protestantism had become an established religion in many European countries and this precipitated the emergence of a wave of non-conformist Protestant sects that challenged the new orthodoxy, particularly in England. These groups, for example, the Quakers, Shakers, Methodists, and Puritans, stressed individual religious experience, the importance of scripture and reasserted an apocalyptic vision as a means to 'reclaim' Protestantism from what was characterised as the 'apostasy' of the established churches. This apocalyptic vision took the form of Post-Tribulation, Pre-millennialism. The re-emergence of apocalypticism between the late eighteenth and mid-nineteenth centuries is not coincidental (McGinn, 1994). Non-conformists saw the events of the French and American Revolutions (both events that appeared as triumphs of secularism over religion) as epoch ending; that is they seemed to be signalling the end of one era and the start of another. The rise of Science and the onset of modernisation also seemed to signal a new era, which embraced attacks on religion, faith, tradition and so forth; to non-conformist Protestants this looked like the 'Tribulation' was occurring. In Europe, non-conformists were persecuted and marginalised; thus, their ideas on the end of the world failed to become widespread, particularly in nations where a state church could reassert orthodoxy. However, in the USA more fertile ground for such beliefs was found, and they would become embedded within North American Protestantism.

Protestant Apocalypticism in the USA

Apocalypticism has always been a central aspect of American versions of Protestantism, particularly conservative ones. Indeed, as was noted in Chapter 3, revivalism was a key feature of nineteenth century American Protestantism. North American Protestantism has always had a strong millennialist belief for a number of reasons that inter-link (Ahlstrom, 1975, Noll, 1992). Firstly, the characteristics of American Protestantism, such as its non-conformity and lack of denominationalism, allow it to embrace ideas that established churches would suppress. Secondly, the belief in a 'chosen' nation with a 'chosen' people, held by most American Protestants, lends itself to apocalypticism, in that such a status is predicated partly on a destiny, an outcome. The re-emergence of millennialism was partly prompted by the French and American Revolutions where socio-political events, both of which represented great breaks with the past, became interpreted as 'signs' of the Biblically foretold 'Tribulation'. The seeming triumph of secularism in both those revolutions added weight to the interpretation that a new age was dawning and one that would be 'godless'. The 'Great Awakenings' that spread through the nation between the War of Independence and the Civil War were fuelled by millennialism and the belief that this new nation, founded by Protestants should usher in a new form of 'pure' faith. Prophecy movements, such as the Millerites, became popular and increasingly scripture was studied for apocalyptic 'signs'. At this time millennialism was a positive vision, which viewed the USA as a new dawn, a 'chosen' nation full of hope and optimism (Noll, 1992). However, this vision became increasingly apocalyptic by the end of the nineteenth century.

By the end of the nineteenth century the impact of modernisation, secularism and mass immigration had started to challenge the long-standing White, Protestant hegemony of the USA (Ahlstrom, 1975). The optimistic millennialism of earlier periods shifted into a darker apocalyptic vision of a nation whose soul was in jeopardy. For fundamentalist Protestants the rapid social and cultural changes sweeping the northern states in the nineteenth century, were 'signs' that the end was fast approaching and that a period of 'Tribulation' was at hand. The social consequences of urbanisation, such as rising crime and disease, alongside the spread of secularism and liberalism certainly generated appropriate apocalyptic imagery (Marsden, 1980). The most popular form of pre-millennialism was Dispensational Pre-millennialism, which had been first outlined by John Nelson Darby in the 1830s. This approach sees the re-establishment of Israel as a crucial 'sign' that the end of the world approaches. It holds the view that Christ will return immediately before a seven year worldwide 'Tribulation'. Jesus will take all 'true' believers up to Heaven by means of a 'Rapture', leaving the 'fallen' behind to suffer through the 'Tribulation' years, when the Anti-Christ gains power. The 'Tribulation' ends in the final battle between 'good' and 'evil', with the armies of the former led by Jesus and his saints. This is followed by the 'Second Coming' of Jesus to lead the church which reigns for a millennium before the 'Last Judgement' occurs. This new interpretation of existing pre-millennial visions placed a greater emphasis on the 'chosen' few who would literally be swept up in the 'Rapture', which could happen at any time. Dispensationalism also places greater emphasis on the prediction of dates for the end-time events, as well as on discerning 'signs' of the end. Dispensationalism was popularised via the Schofield Reference Bible, a standard text for most conservative Protestants in the USA (McGinn, 1994, Marsden, 1980). Dispensationalism became popular partly because it added a sense of immediacy to prevailing apocalyptic visions; things could literally happen at any time and this fed into fundamentalist views that time was running out to save the 'soul' of the nation from the onslaught of modernity and its incumbent foes of secularism and liberalism. In addition, the preoccupation with 'signs' gave a focus for fundamentalists' apocalyptic energy and offered validation for their sense of urgency.

Apocalypticism and Being 'Chosen'

Apocalypticism frames a worldview based on an identity of 'being chosen'; it gives it validation and agency. As was noted in Chapter 5, why be 'chosen' if there is no greater cosmological purpose or reward? End-time beliefs provide this sense of purpose or reward. Apocalypticism places the 'chosen' centre stage in a greater divine plan and shows them the consequences or end products of their commitment to orthodoxy and orthopraxy. A view in an imminent end of the world also lends a sense of urgency to fundamentalist struggles to 'save' the 'soul' of the nation and therefore energises their political campaigning: the cosmic clock is literally ticking.

McGinn (1994) and Boyer (1992) both emphasise the role that apocalyptic rhetoric has played throughout western culture in shaping, interpreting and processing socio-political struggles and periods of conflict and strife. Such rhetoric draws heavily upon Biblical apocalyptic scriptures and allows groups to think through 'meaning crisis' events through recourse to a pre-existing meaning framework with identifiable 'villains', events, 'signs' and results. Such rhetoric is highly interpretative of scriptures (which are nevertheless deemed to be literal) and thus is flexible and can be applied to newly emerging scenarios with ease; both Boyer (1992) and McGinn (1994) illustrate the differing historical contexts and events that have precipitated the use of apocalyptic rhetoric. To illustrate the following passage from the *Book of Isaiah* has been used to refer to both nuclear war and global warming as possible scenarios for the end of the world:

> And the stream thereof shall be turned into pitch, and the dust thereof into brimstone, and the land thereof shall become burning pitch.

> It shall not be quenched night nor day, the smoke thereof shall go up for ever: from generation to generation it shall lie waste: none shall pass through it for ever and ever (Isaiah 34: 9–10).

At its heart such rhetoric has a basic message to rally communities that perceive themselves to be under threat, whether real or imagined: God is on our side, we will prevail and our 'enemies' will be punished (McGinn, 1994). This is a powerful message and remains a potent socio-political tool for religious groups (such as fundamentalists) and secular groups (a good example is the use of apocalyptic imagery in many environmental campaigns of the past decade) alike. As fundamentalism emerged as a reaction to and a critique of modernity, it is hardly surprising that the consequences of modernisation should be interpreted as 'signs' of the coming 'Tribulation' and that apocalyptic rhetoric be widely used to rally fundamentalist (and other conservative protestants) to action against what was perceived to be a threat to their cultural and religious identities. It allowed early fundamentalists to couch their struggle as beyond the level of secular political concerns and attach it to a wider divine framework.

Apocalyptic rhetoric remains a key aspect of Protestant fundamentalism today, partly prompted by the establishment of the state of Israel in 1948. For Dispensationalists the re-establishment of the state of Israel is seen as a key 'sign' that the end of the world is starting and the 'Rapture' will soon occur. Similarly, the founding of the European Union has been taken as a 'sign' that the former Roman Empire has been re-established; another marker of the coming 'Tribulation'. Likewise the year 2000 and the two Gulf Wars have been viewed as 'signs', the latter having great significance due to their geographical location, close to the Holy Land. In the 1970s Hal Lindsey's *The Late Great Planet Earth* was one of the biggest selling novels of the decade and introduced Dispensationalism to a new generation of fundamentalists. The leaders of the fundamentalist revival of the 1970s and 1980s, such as Jerry Falwell, were also popularisers of Dispensationalism. In the 1980s and 1990s, Tim Lahaye's *Left Behind* series of books became even more popular than the work of Lindsey, selling over sixty three million copies in the USA alone; now there is even a computer game based on the novels aimed at fundamentalist children so that they can 'play out' the end of the world. By the turn of the Second Millennium apocalypticism was fully marketed by and to fundamentalist communities through 'end of the world' tours of the Holy Land, a plethora of websites offering advice and survival equipment (for example, www. raptureready.com), and a range of 'Rapture Ready' merchandise from bumper stickers to countdown watches. According to a Time/CNN poll in 2002, fifty nine per cent of Americans believed that the events outlined in the *Book of Revelation* will take place.

God's Way community had several volumes by both Lindsey and LaHaye in their communal library, which they saw as commentaries on what was wrong with the secular world and in agreement with their own worldview. However, they shied away from other more consumerist apocalypticism, but did participate in local Prophecy meetings where end-time, specifically sign-interpretation, was the focus of discussion.

Looking for 'Signs'

The interpretation and identification of 'signs' is a key aspect of Apocalypticism; they literally signpost the key end of the world events and raise apocalyptic awareness among communities. The instrumental act of locating and interpreting 'signs' also channels the socio-political energies of social groups and gives a broader meaning (and vindication) to their lives, particularly in relation to their oppositional view of the world (McGinn, 1994).

God's Way community were founded in part through an apocalyptic vision that their founder Abraham Zion had during a coma; this vision had convinced him of their important God-given role and future destiny. Therefore a belief in the end of the world is a key component of their worldview; essentially it validates their sense of 'being chosen', in that they have a post-apocalyptic destiny that is theirs alone. God's Way's members view the belief in the 'Rapture' held by most other fundamentalists as more open to question than literal; they are unsure as to whether anyone but them will be spared the end of the world. Although members often confessed (in private) that they hoped 'true believers' that they knew within their locale might be 'saved' as they were 'good people'. God's Way, like all protestant fundamentalists, are preoccupied with 'signs', although they have the advantage in that God informed Abraham that the final 'sign' of the end of time was the spontaneous combustion of their communal Bible and the *Books of Abraham*. However as this will be the last 'sign'; it remains important for them to locate other 'signs' that establish a time-scale. God's Way community approach this in the manner of the majority of the fundamentalist community, by linking specific trends, events and people back to Biblical apocalyptic texts.

The basic apocalyptic framework of events and people as foretold in the Bible predicates a period of 'Tribulation' (usually seven years long) where the Anti-Christ will gain power over the world. Although believers maintain that they will be 'Raptured' just as the 'Tribulation' starts; they still need to locate when it is beginning so that they might anticipate their 'Rapture'. In a sense there is a period where the secular world experiences such moral decay that it reaches a 'tipping point' whereby the 'Tribulation' inevitably occurs, as this will be the optimum environment for the Anti-Christ to prosper and gain ascendancy. Therefore a range of events are taken as 'signs' that this 'tipping point' is almost upon us.

There are three key categories of events that are interpreted in this way; firstly, major political events relating to the Middle East, particularly conflicts. This is due to interpretations of Biblical scripture that identify the final battle of 'Armageddon' occurring in the Holy Land, as well as prophecies that talk of the significance of the 'East'. Of course this region is also the provenance of the Bible, Jesus and the *Old Testament* prophets and therefore has a specific role to play at the end of the world. Thus the founding of the state of Israel in 1948, the enlargement of the European Union in the 1990s, the two Gulf Wars, the ongoing Israeli-Palestinian conflict, 9/11 and the threat of Islamist terrorism in general, are all significant 'signs' that the countdown has begun or is close. Secondly, national social trends, particularly relating to moral issues, such as the rise in divorce, abortion, single parents, and STI rates; the increasing normalisation of homosexuality; working mothers; crime statistics; growing drug and alcohol abuse, and so forth are all seen as 'signs' that there is widespread social and moral decay. Thirdly, there are natural events, such as Hurricane Katrina, recent Tsunamis, long-term droughts, increasingly wild weather patterns. Most secular commentators would attribute such phenomena to the impact of Global Warming. However, fundamentalists are literalists and few 'believe' in Global warming; rather such extreme weather is a 'sign' of the end.

The members of God's Way community would scan newspaper headlines to show evidence of such 'signs' from crime rates to bad weather. Isaac Zion, their current leader, would read out such headlines at the end of the nightly communal meal and say 'God's sure showin' us the way thur'. This was always greeted with whoops of joy and sometimes applause. Fundamentalists welcome conflict in the Middle East as they see this as a means to precipitate the start of the end of the world. Indeed throughout the late 1990s and particularly in 1999 the Israeli authorities had a constant struggle to control and remove fundamentalist Christians intent on provoking conflict with Arabs in order to start the countdown to end-time (LaCayo, 1999). 'Rapture Ready' websites often feature countdown clocks linked to specific events or phenomena, each one bringing the final hour closer. For example, www.raptureready.com has a 'Rapture Index' which rises according to such events; it currently hovers around the one hundred and sixty mark meaning it is time to 'fasten your seatbelts' the 'Rapture' is coming soon. Biblical scriptures, such as the *Book of Revelation*, identify moral and social decay, wars, famines and plagues as all 'signs' of the 'Tribulation'. By linking a range of phenomena, the evidence can appear overwhelming to literalists who overlook all other interpretations. Such 'sign' spotting also reinforces and seeks to validate the apocalyptic worldview, while also offering an explanatory framework with which to make sense of often complex socio-political conflicts.

The other key apocalyptic figure is that of the Anti-Christ who appears as the 'Tribulation' occurs and whose rise to power pushes the world fully into the 'Tribulation' period. The *Book of Revelation* is the main source of 'information' on this figure, who is usually depicted as male, deeply charismatic, a leader, and someone who offers false leadership. The original Anti-Christ from the *Book of Revelation* is clearly the Emperor Nero, arch persecutor of the early Christians. Since then this figure has been attributed by religious and secular apocalypticists, to a range of individuals through history, including various Popes, Napoleon, Hitler, and more recently Ronald Reagan and George W. Bush (Boyer, 1992, McGinn, 1994). More recently Barack Obama has been identified as a possible Anti-Christ figure by many on the 'Religious Right'. His race, 'foreign' name, Muslim father, overseas childhood, seeming apologia towards Islam, state interventionist plans, especially on healthcare, and his savvy use of the Internet as a campaign tool all meet the 'criteria' of a figure who is 'the lightening cometh out of the east' (St Matthew 24: 24–27), who seeks to take over the world and is highly charismatic. The Internet has long been viewed with suspicion by fundamentalists as a key resource for the Anti-Christ and his minions. *Isaiah* chapter 34, verse 1, which says 'come near, ye nations, to hear, and hearken, ye people: let the earth hear, and all that is therein the world, and all things that come forth of it' is often interpreted as referring to the Internet. Obama's liberalism and racial heritage make him a ready-made figure for demonisation. The Anti-Christ is typically viewed as a man of great power, either politically or economically, which feeds into fundamentalist distrust of politicians and Big business alike.

Apocalypticism often feeds into conspiracy theories, as can be seen among far right militias in the USA who identify government, business and other vested interests working together for their own ends, usually with the outcome to create some form of world government or 'New World Order' (Knight, 2000). Many fundamentalists, including God's Way community, share this view that key politicians were working across nations to form international alliances for their own interests; thus they distrusted the United Nations, European Union and any other form of trans-national alliances. Such groupings were viewed as playing into the hands of the Anti-Christ who would use them to seize absolute power. In Tim LaHaye's *Left Behind* series of books, the Anti-Christ becomes the Secretary-General of the United Nations and uses his position to wield ultimate power. Lahaye views the United Nations as an 'anti-Christian' organisation and based his novel on Biblical scriptures that he claims show that the 'Tribulation' is an era of world government. God's Way community, in common with a wide variety of other conspiracy theory believers (Knight, 2000) believed that bar-codes and magnetic strips on money and swipe cards were all means for the government (and possibly the Anti-Christ) to track the population and control them. They viewed the Internet in a similar way and thus refused to have a computer in the community.

The *Book of Revelation* (specifically Revelation 14:1) identifies the Anti-Christ as being identified by the '666' symbol. Sometimes this can be taken literally in the form of a tattoo or a birthmark; thus President Gorbachev of the USSR's birthmark was seen as a potential 'sign' (Boyer, 1992). More commonly the '666' is seen as more symbolic and numerological systems are often used to uncover the 'true' meaning of an individual's name. The Hebrew system of every letter having a numerical value is the most commonly used (Boyer, 1992). God's Way community tended to avoid trying to identify who the Anti-Christ was, merely saying that 'we'll know soon enough'. But they did view politicians, such as President Clinton or leaders of business, such as Donald Trump, as 'minions'; 'doing the Devil's work for him'. What they meant by that phrase is that liberal politicians and businessmen were intent on spreading social and moral decay and placing the worship of money above all else. Identifying who the Anti-Christ might be or who his 'minions' are, allows fundamentalists to focus their energies on specific political targets who they can then demonise in order to motivate and energise their own communities to political action. In much the same way that the post-revolution, Iranian administration demonised the USA as 'the Great Satan' in order to channel anti-western feeling and further their critique of the Shah's government (Salehi, 1998).

Counting Down

Fundamentalists look for and strive to interpret 'signs' as a means to establish whether the apocalyptic clock has literally started counting down. As the end-time sequence of events is already established via Biblical scriptures, the identification of 'signs' places pressure on believers to identify the date for key events or indeed the very end of the world. The history of apocalyptic belief is littered with failed endings to the world (McGinn, 1994). Claiming exact dates is a high risk strategy for any religious group as it poses the problem of how does that group's meaning system deal with the inevitable 'meaning crisis' encountered when the end does not come (Festinger et al., 1964). The majority of groups fail to survive such an encounter with prophecy failure, unless the power of individual charismatic leaders prevails (Festinger, 1964). The more effective approach is for groups to avoid naming exact dates but rather to imply that 'the time is near' and that God will soon reveal all.

God's Way community adopt this position of seeing the 'signs gathering' to imply the end is near, but view the mystery of the date as appropriate because it is in 'God's careful hands'. Sarah Zion put it as 'we'll know what's gonna happen when he decides an' that's that'. They viewed the exact naming of dates as 'blasphemous'. However, throughout their history dates had been named as 'possible' (based on a reading of the 'signs') and when the date passed without event it was viewed as 'God's just testin us'. Isaac Zion, the current leader, saw the postponement of such dates as a 'test' for the 'chosen' from God. The community anticipate the end of the world; they literally cannot wait for it and so they view postponements as God 'testing' them for lapses in behaviour. In other words, they are not yet ready for their apocalyptic 'reward' and must continue to 'suffer' living in the secular world that they despise. A similar view is held across the Protestant fundamentalist community, where the 'Rapture' is viewed as the culmination of belief and a joyous occasion; one that is hotly anticipated (Carpenter, 1997). Countdown clocks and watches are commonly used by fundamentalists and numerous 'Rapture Ready' websites have countdown meters. It is also the reason why the Christian Right is so hawkish in foreign policy, particularly around intervention in the Middle East; such action might, literally, kick-start the end of the world (Boyer, 1992). This makes fundamentalists difficult political opponents as they have nothing to lose in this world and everything to gain from the next.

Apocalyptic Agency

Apocalyptic rhetoric and beliefs throughout history has been a useful socio-political tool for a wide range of groups and communities (McGinn, 1994); it continues to do so among Protestant fundamentalists. It serves a number of uses for such communities. Firstly, it validates that group's worldview by showing them the outcome of their orthodoxy and orthopraxy. Secondly, it reinforces and validates their view of 'being chosen' by providing an ultimate goal or direction for this status. Thirdly, it provides agency for all socio-political action by linking it to worldview, identity and also the belief that as 'chosen', God is on side. It also adds urgency to political action by literally implying that the clock is ticking and that time is of the essence. Finally it offers an interpretative framework for often complex socio-political issues through the identification of 'signs' and 'enemies' that can be validated via scriptural interpretation. This makes fundamentalists strong political opponents who can draw on a ready-made apocalyptic literature to communicate political messages, alongside an often elaborate demonisation of political foes, which is also framed by apocalyptic scripture.

Apocalypticism presents a heady message that life and society can and will change, which makes it an attractive belief for communities who feel marginalised from the mainstream. Its ability to frame and explain events and place them in a fixed Biblical context adds to its attractiveness, particularly for Biblical literalists; while the focus on counting down and becoming 'Rapture Ready' gives an instrumental and directed focus for individuals and communities who may feel buffeted by social changes that create and then amplify their feelings of marginalisation (McGinn, 1994, Marsden, 1980, Boyer, 1992). Protestant fundamentalists generally perceive themselves to be marginalised in the USA; a nation they view as intrinsically 'theirs' (Ammerman, 1991).

The popularity of 'end time' books such as *The Late, Great Planet Earth* by Hal Lindsey and Tim LaHaye's *Left Behind* series, present the mainstream fundamentalist apocalyptic worldview, but link it to current socio-political issues and contexts, such as, ongoing conflict in the Middle East. This makes these books powerful not just as populisers of fundamentalist, Pre-millennialism, but as disseminators of powerful political messages that are directly sympathetic to the Religious Right. For example, its distrust of trans-national organisations like the United Nations and European Union or its fear of 'big' government. Thus such texts, alongside apocalypticism in other formats, such as film, television and computer games, are a source of politicisation for many communities who might otherwise have avoided secular political concerns, particularly issues with an international context.

The use of apocalyptic rhetoric to identify and demonise political foes, particularly through the figure of the Anti-Christ (and his minions) also feeds into the 'othering' process that fundamentalists, like God's Way community, engage in as part of their belief in a special status (Scott, 1996). The 'fallen', the opposite of the 'chosen', are those who will be duped by the Anti-Christ and his minions and are portrayed as easily fooled by politicians and businessmen; they are also easily enthralled by celebrities. This portrayal of the 'fallen' serves to demonise them and also constructs their important role as 'other' to the 'chosen'. One aspect of this construction is the view that the 'fallen' live in a world that is close to the 'tipping point' into the 'Tribulation' and thus a world that is dangerous and potentially damaging for the 'chosen'. This means that special measures must be taken when navigating the secular world. One consequence of this is that Protestant fundamentalists are oppositional in their view of the world around them and seek to maintain strong levels of separateness, from those they classify as 'fallen'.

Chapter 7
'Us or Them': An Oppositional Worldview

All worldviews present their view of reality as the 'taken-for-granted' interpretation of the social world (Berger and Luckmann, 1966). This leads to behaviours that often privilege our interpretation of the world over others, for example, ethnocentrism (Berger and Luckmann, 1966, Said, 1978). In a sense all worldviews are potentially in opposition to each other and threaten social consensus. However such privileging can be challenged and interpretations changed, often through engagement with alternative perspectives. It could be argued that this is essential for the health of a society and a means to facilitate social innovation and change (Berger and Luckmann, 1966, Lukes, 1985). This is particularly the case in modern or late modern societies where worldviews draw on scientific and other secular knowledge forms. Indeed late modernity is characterised as an era of increasing acceptance of competing views of reality as demonstrated in the prevalence of cultural and moral relativism (Giddens, 1991, Beck et al., 1994).

Historically, religious worldviews made claims to ultimate authority but even these had to actively suppress challenges and ultimately, accommodate them (Berger, 1967). In the mainstream and liberal wings of the world's religions, worldviews merge religious and secular visions of reality. The fundamentalist worldview is one that operates beyond the level of mere cultural chauvinism that presumes an epistemological and ontological superiority, but rather it claims to be *the* ultimate view of reality. It is constructed in opposition to all other competing interpretations of reality, particularly the secular-liberal consensus that predominates in most western societies. This oppositionality characterises this worldview and directs fundamentalists' view of and engagement with the world outside of their communities. The degree of oppositionality is amplified by other aspects of their worldview, particularly their belief in a forthcoming apocalypse that categorises the world into those who will be 'saved' and those who will perish; an issue that was explored in the previous chapter. Living a strictly religious life, built on orthodoxy and orthopraxy also aids the demarcation of the world into 'chosen' and 'fallen'.

It is hardly surprising that such an oppositional worldview should entail high levels of discriminatory behaviour, including sexism, racism and homophobia. Psychological tests (see for example, Altemeyer and Hunsberger, 1992, Hunsberger, 1995 and 1996, Laythe et al., 2001, Laythe et al., 2002, Altemeyer, 2003) reveal a strong tendency towards prejudice and discrimination, particularly racism and homophobia, among religious fundamentalists of both Christian and non-Christian backgrounds. This is hardly surprising given that this is a worldview that is built upon discrimination via the strong identification of 'right' and wrong' behaviours and 'right' and 'wrong' socio-cultural groups; one would expect fundamentalists to 'test 'positively' for such behaviours. Clearly, this is a worldview which would not be expected to show a high level of tolerance towards cultural diversity or relativism, and Protestant fundamentalism increasing growth and political mobilisation in the past forty years, during a period when society has embraced plurality and relativism, shows this to be the case.

'Chosen' and 'Fallen'

This book argues that the central element of the fundamentalist worldview is the belief in 'being chosen' or 'called'. This belief establishes a set of behaviours and beliefs that are viewed as the 'right' or 'true' ones. In turn these beliefs and behaviours reinforce the sense of 'being chosen'. However a belief in 'being chosen' necessitates the existence of a contrastive identity; an 'other' that is not 'chosen'. Without this 'other' it would be difficult to maintain this extraordinary claim to uniqueness, particularly in a modern, secular nation such as the USA. For fundamentalists this 'other' are usually labelled the 'fallen', although other labels might be used, such as the 'unbelievers', 'the lost' or 'false believers'.

God's Way community use the term the 'fallen', as did their fundamentalist neighbours. The 'fallen', unsurprisingly, are everything that the 'chosen' are not: immoral, unfaithful, destructive, evil, non-believers, greedy, lazy, gullible, and most important of all 'lost' in that they cannot see the bigger, divine, scheme of things and therefore the 'fallen' are also 'damned'. The important role of 'others' in reinforcing claims to cultural or religious uniqueness was discussed in Chapter 4 so these issues will not be revisited here. Suffice to say that 'others' are social constructions that operate to reinforce the specialness of one group over another and that 'othering' is ideological in that it is usually used to justify socio-political actions (Arens, 1980, Said, 1978). This is certainly the case with Protestant fundamentalists who use the 'fallen' as a key element in the identification and demonisation of political targets; something that will be explored in greater detail in the next chapter.

The 'fallen' are defined in relation to what they are not, that is 'chosen', and so the 'fallen' are a useful means to facilitate the construction, validation and reinforcement of the fundamentalist worldview. At a basic level the 'fallen' operate to symbolise and mark out all that the 'chosen' are in opposition to ;all that the 'fallen are not. Thus they facilitate identity construction. The 'fallen' and their perceived behaviour and beliefs act to validate the orthodoxy and orthopraxy of everyday fundamentalist life, at a level that even the youngest fundamentalist can understand. For example, in God's Way community the children would draw cartoons depicting the 'fallen' and the consequences of their 'wicked' actions. Their cartoons, typically, showed African Americans, suited businessmen, and Jews; gambling, drinking, murdering, and indulging in a wide range of deviant acts. Such pictures were highly praised by the adults and periodically pinned to the walls of the communal dining hall. This pictorial theology lesson was highly effective.

Similarly, the 'fallen' reinforce the role that the 'chosen' will play at the end of the world; without them there is no real reward awaiting the 'chosen' that can be contrasted with the eternal punishment that awaits the 'fallen'. The 'fallen' also play a key role in apocalyptic events, where their mass 'immorality' helps usher in the 'Tribulation' and their communal gullibility allows the Anti-Christ to gain power. They also have a final apocalyptic role in demonstrating what happens to 'unbelievers', that is, they will suffer eternal punishment by God. The 'fallen' also operate as a mass morality lesson in what happens when you deviate from the 'true' path. Finally, the 'fallen' serve as useful targets of the wider fundamentalist critique of modernity and its incumbent evils of secularism and liberalism. Ironically, the 'chosen' cannot live without the 'fallen'.

Who Are the 'Fallen?

Fundamentalists, like God's way community, typically use the blanket label of 'fallen' to refer to all those who are not identified as part of their actual community of faith. However, on closer inspection, there is a hierarchy of 'fallen', and within this seeming absolute dichotomy, many contradictions are at work. Similarly many obvious targets are overlooked. The 'fallen' fall into a number of categories: non-whites; 'immorals'; liberals; false believers, secularists; and urban dwellers, which can differ in emphasis across regions (Bruce, 2008, Ammerman, 1993, Carpenter, 1997, Harding, 2000). Often one 'fallen' individual might 'fit' into more than one category, thus President Clinton was viewed by God's Way community as liberal, secular and 'immoral'. President Obama might be viewed as fitting all but the secularist category.

African Americans

There are significant levels of racism among White, protestant fundamentalists, especially in the southern states (Ammerman, 1991), although openly racist statements are less prevalent than homophobic ones; reflecting changing views of race, but not necessarily sexuality. Biblical references are often used to justify the separation of the races and prohibit the idea of 'mixed marriage'. The 'peoples of the Book' (i.e. the Bible) are seen as White and there is a strong discourse that associates whiteness with being 'chosen' by God or at least closer to God. This racism partly accounts for African Americans' inclusion in the 'fallen' category. However, as previously discussed, the association of 'chosen' status with whiteness is deeply embedded in White Protestants' sense of religico-national identity: their ancestors are seen as the 'true' founders and builders of the USA (Ahlstrom, 1975). God's Way community, although none of the community's members had an American heritage that went farther back than the post-Civil War era, all claimed a link back to the 'Pilgrim Fathers'. They enthusiastically celebrated 'Thanksgiving' every November with the children re-enacting the landing at Plymouth Rock and the founding of the first Puritan settlements. In their re-enactment of the first 'Thanksgiving', Native Americans hand over the nation (as well as the corn and turkeys) to the leader of the settlers and accept the 'true' faith. It ends with one of the settlers predicting that one day a great leader called 'Abraham' will emerge to 'save' the nation, as the Biblical Abraham 'saved' the ancient Jews. God's Way community's members viewed African Americans as prone to depravity and weaker, physically and morally, citing high rates of illegitimacy, abortion, drug addiction, alcoholism, welfare dependency and incarceration as evidence to support this view. They also identified whiteness as an attribute of the ancient Jews who had created the *Old Testament* on which their faith was partly founded; therefore they equated whiteness with the 'true' people of faith.

The community's view of African Americans also reflects their regional context, demonstrating the importance of contextualising different fundamentalist groups in order to understand their specific selection of 'others'. Ninety per cent of the population of their home state is White, and the Black population were overwhelmingly found in the two large urban centres of their Missouri. These two main cities are in the national top ten for welfare payments and twelfth for violent crime. African Americans are more likely to be recipients of welfare and be perpetrators (and victims) of crime. Most citizens of their home state live in urban centres and there exists a tension between the rural farming areas in the south, and the urban, manufacturing areas in the north. This tension focuses on race, where the Black population are blamed for 'draining' regional resources due to their lack of 'self sufficiency', reliance on 'hand outs' (i.e. welfare payments) and the cost to 'keeping 'em locked away'; the latter a reference to the high percentage of African Americans in state prisons. African Americans were also seen as adding to the moral and social 'decay' of the state, through their higher levels of family breakdown, alcoholism, delinquency, drug abuse, and illegitimacy. Their perceived dependency on welfare was attributed to ethnic laziness. Often the community's members (and indeed their neighbours) invoked imagery of African Americans as vermin, who 'breed like rats' and 'you can never get 'em out of your house'. The symbolism of a rat also conjures up imagery around dirt, a lack of hygiene and being carriers of disease; again these elements were invoked by God's Way's members in talking about African Americans in their home state. In the most extreme instance, Isaac Zion, described the growing Black population as a 'plague wrought upon us'.

Such views of African Americans were always juxtaposed against a rural community facing rising bankruptcy for small farmers who 'had worked hard all their lives, asking for nuthin', as one member put it. For God's Way community, who faced economic hardship themselves as small farmers, identified with the plight of their farming neighbours, irrespective of their beliefs (albeit most were also conservative Protestants). The state government was seen as elected by and for urban dwellers (read here African Americans) and intrinsically 'corrupt', both morally and politically. Reports in the local Christian newspaper of attacks on African Americans in the area, which were quite commonplace, were greeted with nods of approval from community members, particularly older members, who remembered 'when niggers knew their place'. The community saw such attacks as a means to keep their home county Whites-only or as Sarah Zion put it to 'keep the dirt from spreading and getting in'. Thus, as an 'other' African Americans serve to symbolise and reinforce the community's view of cities, 'Big' government, and their racial identity.

Jews

Although God's Way community identified the whiteness of the ancient Jews as part justification for their racist views in relation to African Americans; they did not see Jews as a 'chosen' people. They considered Jews to have once been the 'chosen' people but that they had since lost their status. Instead Jews were now 'fallen' due to their failure to recognise Jesus as the Messiah, and also because of a perception of Jewish influence in government, business and the arts that was seen as promulgating Liberalism and Secularism. The idea of a Jewish conspiracy to take control of government has been a recurring belief in Europe, and more recently, the USA, for the past two thousand years, where it has fuelled Anti-Semitism in various guises and nations (McGinn, 1994, Knight, 1999).

On the community bus, when driving back from farm labouring, the bus radio would tune into a Christian station that had a daily 'spot the Jew' slot. This radio game involved a range of celebrities, musicians, actors and politicians being 'outed' as Jews. The community's members enjoyed this show and cited it as evidence of the 'Jewish conspiracy' at the heart of the nation. Jews therefore fall into the category of 'false believers'. The community depicted Jews as 'lazy', 'fat', often homosexual, prone to left-wing political beliefs, rich, and 'plotters' who seek to 'steal from under us, what God took from them'. Jews were often used as a 'morality tale' by Isaac of what happens when the 'chosen' people of God do not follow the 'true way'. He would then recount how Jews have been punished by God, not just by losing their 'special' status, but through events like the Holocaust; 'God could've stopped him [Hitler] but he had been angered'. Jews are an 'other' who serves to demonstrate to the community's members what happens when the 'chosen' do not follow God's will; they serve as a reminder of the fragile nature of being 'chosen'. Again significant levels of Anti-Semitism can be seen throughout Protestant fundamentalism in the USA, although the state of Israel is seen as important in terms of end-time mythology (McGinn, 1994, Bruce, 2008). Although the state of Israel itself is often lauded for its tough stance on the Islamic world, this support is not necessarily extended to the American Jewish community. Similarly the Religious Right support Israel and Israeli military action in the Middle East, but typically due to a view that it might lead to a final conflict between Arab and Jew that might precipitate the end of the world.

Hispanic Americans

God's Way community members also categorised Hispanic Americans as 'fallen', despite never coming across any in their locale. They based their view on two key points. Firstly, they rightly associated Hispanic culture with Catholicism, a religion that the community saw as 'fallen' and one which had throughout history perverted the 'true' message of Jesus. Antagonism towards Catholicism has been an aspect of Protestantism since the Reformation and anti-Catholic feelings are common among conservative Protestants generally and fundamentalists specifically (Lindberg, 2005, Bruce, 2008, Carpenter, 1997). Secondly, the community did not approve of the growing political power of the Hispanic community, especially on the issue of bilingualism. In the 1990s there was a growing movement to place bilingualism at the heart of the nation, best exemplified by the use of bilingual signs, which are now commonplace throughout the USA, particularly in areas with large Spanish speaking communities, such as California. The issue of language is complicated by the fact that the Constitution does not decree that Americans should speak a specific language; although tradition has established English as the nation's chosen language. Political conservatives in the 1990s, including the Religious Right, sought to amend the Constitution to establish English as the official national language. This movement failed, but conservatives remain resistant to bilingualism. For Protestant fundamentalists the founders of the nation were not only White Protestants but also English speakers, therefore the 'true' American is one who speaks English as a first language. Hence the 'chosen' also speak English (and are white).

God's Way community based their views of Hispanic Americans on media reporting and depiction. They saw them as 'foreigners' who had 'crept' over the border from Mexico (they viewed all Hispanic Americans as Mexican in origin) and who were determined to 'make us all talk Spanish'. When they read about bilingual signs they saw this as evidence that the country was 'being given away' by those in power and seemed incredulous that such signs existed in their nation. For them, Hispanic Americans are the 'other' who demonstrate the cultural destructiveness of cultural plurality and relativism, which religious conservatives of all backgrounds dislike and associate with their twin 'enemies' of Liberalism and Secularism (Ammerman, 1991, Bruce, 2008).

Native Americans

Despite obviously racist views towards African, Jewish and Hispanic Americans, God's Way community's members showed a certain reverence for Native Americans. Although their 'Thanksgiving' play shows Native Americans handing over the nation; the community saw Native Americans as 'noble' keepers of the nation before the 'chosen' arrived. They also considered Native Americans' ability to 'live in harmony with God's creation' as something to be respected and admired. The communal library had many books on Native American culture and skills, and the children were encouraged to learn about such culture. Thus, Native Americans occupied a category of 'other' that operated outside of the 'chosen'/'fallen' dichotomy. They served to illustrate to the community's members that God's Creation was sufficient for 'all life's needs', but more importantly they served to demonstrate the power of humility, in their 'handing over' of the 'chosen' nation to the 'chosen' people (i.e. White, Protestants). Such positive views of Native American culture are not necessarily shared across the Protestant fundamentalist community, where the former are more likely to be associated with alcohol abuse and gambling, both pursuits that would place them in a 'fallen' category.

'False Believers'

Both Jews and Catholics are placed in the category of 'false believers', alongside all Protestants who are not fundamentalists. Catholicism has long been viewed with distrust by conservative Protestants, who view it as a religion of 'apostasy', which corrupted the original message of Jesus and the *Old Testament* prophets (Barr, 1977). God's Way community believed that God himself had warned their leader Abraham, via a vision, that Catholicism had so 'corrupted' the *New Testament* through mistranslation and misinterpretation that it needed to be abandoned as a literal scripture. The community only used the *Book of Revelation* as a literal text from the *New Testament*; the other books were typically avoided. They did not view Catholics as fellow Christians and joked about Catholics 'getting drunk' in church (a reference to Communion wine) and 'worshipping' 'false Gods' (a reference to the veneration of the Virgin Mary and saints). When discussing Catholics, they found them amusing figures that were seen as 'stoopid' for believing and worshipping as they did. Revelations about sexually abusive priests, which first emerged in the USA in the 1990s, and the Church's subsequent 'covering-up' of this abuse, further reinforced God's Way community's view of Catholicism as a 'depraved' and 'corrupted' faith. They delighted in reading about this abuse as it proved to them how 'right Abraham was about 'em'.

In relation to other Protestants, God's Way community would not view evangelical Christians as necessarily 'chosen', especially if they worked in alliance with non-conservative churches. However other fundamentalists would see 'born again' evangelicals as also 'chosen'. This has been a tension within protestant fundamentalism since the 1940s (Barr, 1977, Ammerman, 1991, Marsden, 1980). Yet God's Way community participates in moral campaigns (for example, the pro-life campaign) alongside evangelicals and other conservative Christians, including Catholics, without drawing attention to this contradiction. Liberal Protestants are seen as the worst 'false believers' because they seek to compromise everything they believe, and assist in the deconstruction of faith through adopting Biblical Criticism and ecumenism. This is a view shared by the vast majority of Protestant fundamentalists (Barr, 1977, Carpenter, 1997, Marsden, 1980). The community's members did not view Liberal Protestants as religious at all and did not understand how they could be labelled 'Christians' if they did not believe the Bible as 'God's words'; clearly a reference to Biblical Criticism.

God's Way community showed no awareness of other religions, such as Islam. However the post 9/11 environment has seen fundamentalists demonise Muslims as arch enemies of the USA and therefore definitely 'fallen' (Bruce, 2008). The association of Islam with terrorism is widely held, and the seeming conciliation towards the Arab world by President Obama, has been seen as an example of how the liberal-secular world seeks to capitulate to the 'false believers'. 'False Believers' operate as an 'other' who not only reinforce who is a 'true believer' (and who is not) but also they serve to show how easy it is for people to be fooled into believing what is not 'true'. They are a lesson in gullibility and the consequences of their gullibility are evident in the perception of a 'moral' decline in their own and other communities.

'Immorals'

The category of 'immorals' includes homosexuals as they are not only deemed to subvert God-given gender roles, but also to encourage sexual promiscuity as they cannot have reproductive sex. God's Way community believed that as well as a Jewish conspiracy at the heart of government there was also a 'queer' or 'fag' conspiracy, where leading politicians were 'queers' and encouraged 'queer' rights. For example, they believed that Hillary Clinton was a lesbian who drove her husband to acts of 'sexual immorality' (a reference here to the Lewinsky affair). Thus homosexuality is seen as akin to a disease that spreads and encourages a whole range of 'immoral' sexual behaviours. God's Way community would often use the term 'queer' as a form of abuse, amongst themselves and towards non-members. Homosexuals were stereotyped as sexually promiscuous, lewd, depraved, 'dirty', 'plague-carriers', 'girly', 'secretive', and 'weak'.

The wider Protestant fundamentalist community is rabidly anti-gay (see for example, Exodus International, Homosexuals Anonymous, and NARTH) and homosexuality is a key political issue, particularly in relation to same-sex marriage; something which will be explored in the next chapter. Adulterers, Prostitutes, fornicators, abortionists, women who have abortions, pornographers, sex educators, among others, were also seen by God's Way community as 'immorals'. All of these groups are targeted by the wider Protestant fundamentalist community within their political campaigns to 'save' the 'soul' of the nation (LaHaye, 1980, Harding, 2000). God's Way community's members participate in campaigns relating to stopping sexual immorality, specifically relating to abortion, pornography and sex education in their locale. Sexual immorality goes against their values of monogamous, heterosexual, procreative sex within marriage which is seen as 'proper', 'God given', and verified by scriptural accounts. Anything that violates this model of sex or challenges it is obviously categorised as 'fallen'. Isaac Zion, the current leader of God's Way community, would regularly compare contemporary American society as similar to Sodom and Gomorrah; he would delight in reminding members what happened to those cities when God had had enough of their sexual immorality. Fundamentalists generally share this view and see what they perceive to be rising levels of sin and sexual immorality as further 'sign' that the end-times are near. Sexual immorality is seen as giving in to temptation and being seduced by sin; thus it leaves individuals susceptible to the 'immoral' messages of the Anti-Christ and his followers and so further precipitates the end of the world's approach. Thus 'immorals' serve as an 'other' who not only reinforce the moral uprightness of the 'chosen' but they also operate as targets with which to focus fundamentalist political energies on social-moral issues.

Liberals, Secularists and Humanists

Liberals, secularists and Humanists are also placed in the category of 'fallen'; typically this refers to politicians, educationalists, those involved in the Arts, celebrities and so forth. It can also refer to organisations such as the American Civil Liberties Union (ACLU) and the National Organization for Women (NOW) who champion civil rights and fight inequalities. It is inevitable that those on the 'Religious Right' would be anti-Liberal; the two ideologies are in fundamental opposition to each other politically, culturally and religiously. Liberalism is viewed by fundamentalists as being anti-tradition, anti-religion, and actively promoting moral and cultural pluralism (Marsden, 1980, Ammerman, 1991, Bruce, 2008). Such positions are the antithesis of what fundamentalism stands for; Liberalism is seen as dangerous to American society because it is viewed as inevitably leading to the breakdown of traditional social structures, the spread of 'sexual immorality' and cultural and moral relativism. Many fundamentalists view Liberalism as Anti-American and unpatriotic. Liberals, Secularists and Humanists are viewed synonymously and are perceived to have 'infected' all the major social institutions of the USA, further facilitating the promotion of these viewpoints.

For example, fundamentalists view secular universities as hotbeds of Liberalism and Secularism, and warn against sending their youth to them; this in part led to the establishment of their own higher education institutions, for example Jerry Falwell's Liberty University in Virginia. This can be seen in the literature of the 'Sexual Brokenness' (see for example, Exodus International) and Chastity and Abstinence movements (see for example, True Love Waits) which urge parents to avoid sending their teenagers to secular universities as this will expose them to 'sexual immorality', among other Liberal 'ills'. The public school system with its promotion of sex education, multi-culturalism, and the teaching of evolutionary science are also seen as 'lost' to Liberalism; again this has led to the growing home school movement. The prohibition on prayers in public schools in the 1960s was one of the early catalysts for conservative protestant political activism. God's Way community certainly echoed these views by sending their children to the local fundamentalist run school that had began as a home school, run by a small group of parents who disapproved of what they perceived to be the multi-culturalist and anti-Christian orientation of their local public schools. The two coasts, particularly the east coast were identified as Liberal as was the world of the Arts. The perceived liberalism of the Arts was a main drive behind the so-called 'culture wars' (Hunter, 1992) of the 1980s and 1990s, which will be explored in greater detail in the next chapter. God's Way community did not encounter the world of the Arts beyond the occasional family film on television, preferring to watch and listen to conservative Christian broadcasting; thus they were not that interested in the ongoing 'culture wars'. Often God's Way community, in common with many other protestant fundamentalist groups, merged 'other' categories together; thus Liberal, Secularists were also likely to be Jewish and homosexual. Using the label 'Liberal' or 'Humanist' was not sufficiently demonising and so usually was suffixed by 'they're all fags you know', or 'all Jews are leftie, liberal queers'. This category of 'other' was seen as behind all of society's ills and the eradication of this 'other' was viewed by God's Way as crucial to the 'health' and future of the nation. As an 'other', Liberal-Secularists operate as the 'enemy within', and therefore serve to account for all social problems but also they provide a potential 'solution' through their possible removal.

City Dwellers

Finally, city dwellers are usually categorised as 'fallen' and depictions of the 'Tribulation' are typically set in a large city, often New York. For example, in the computer game of LaHaye's *Left Behind* series the action is played out in a large metropolis. Cities have always been viewed negatively by protestant fundamentalists, and associated with modernisation, immigration, social breakdown and immorality (Marsden, 1980, Scott, 2001). The social and religious decline of the USA, which fundamentalists believe began in the late nineteenth century, started in urban centres, which proved a safe haven for all the communities, competing ideologies and modern ideas that fundamentalists characterise as encouraging social decay (Ammerman, 1991). Much fundamentalist anger towards cities is focused on New York, which is often portrayed as akin to the Biblical Babylon. Abraham Zion, the founder of God's Way community called New York the whore town of Babylon; he associated it with the greatest sin and depravity imaginable. His followers continued to echo this view; for example, Isaac Zion had a photograph of the New York city skyline lit up with a giant lightning bolt which he used to point to and say 'thur a demo of what God will do to 'em'. The negative portrayal of city dwellers is in part predicated on an overly-idealised view of rural America as the 'true', unspoilt, 'authentic' America. As the main fundamentalist heartlands are in the southern and Midwestern states, where agriculture predominates (or did prior to rapid post-World War Two industrialisation and urbanisation), this is hardly surprising (Ammerman, 1991). The association of cities with immigrants, non-Protestants, and non-Whites is also juxtaposed against the association of the farming heartlands as White (protestant) domains. Of course many fundamentalists live in cities, but those that share this view that urban centres as dangerous 'lost' places and maintain strong physical and symbolic boundaries to reduce the potential 'polluting' effect of the city in which they live (Ammerman, 1993).

God's Way community and their neighbouring fundamentalist Protestants view of their state's cities was amplified by their view of vital state resources being swallowed-up by the urban centres, while the sparsely populated rural communities received little assistance. The voting power of the urban centres in contrast to the rural areas, also added to this sense of rural marginalisation, both politically and socially. The fact that city dwellers seemed to have disproportionate voting power and fiscal resources, in contrast to their rural cousins, was seen as evidence that the state government was 'lost' to the 'true' believers. A similar view was held by God's way community in relation to the federal government during the Clinton years, which was seen as supported by and working for the liberal, secular coasts, rather than the rural heartlands. The community, in common with the majority of American conservative Christians had viewed the Reagan years as good for the country in trying to reassert more traditional values. However, Isaac Zion often declared that no secular politician could be fully trusted, because the system of power 'corrupted' and that the only power was 'God's to have and to give'. City dwellers are an 'other' who choose to live in places of 'sin' and are usually associated with other categories of 'fallen', such as 'false believers' or 'immorals'. They serve as future actors in God's Way's apocalyptic vision; reinforce their idealisation of rural America; and most important of all allow the community's members to express their political and social marginalisation.

God's Way community's typology of symbolic 'others' and 'enemies' focuses on their fellow Americans; in other words they rarely discussed wider global issues or viewed other countries or cultures as a 'threat'. Isaac Zion had been the only member of the community to have ever left the USA, which he did during his brief career in the Navy. But it might be presumed that in a post-9/11 environment, God's Way community would gain a greater awareness of Islam and probably feed into the wider Islamophobia prevalent in the conservative Christian community.

Keeping the 'Outside' Out

This typology of 'others' that God's Way community have helps create physical and symbolic boundaries between the world of the 'chosen', and the world of the 'others'. This secular/profane or inside/outside division is commonly found among fundamentalist Protestants. These boundaries are often portrayed as a division between 'purity' and 'pollution'; the 'chosen' living a 'pure' life in contrast to the 'polluting' world of the 'others'. Douglas (1966) noted that the categorisation of 'purity' and 'pollution', particularly in relation to ideas of sacredness, helped establish social and physical boundaries between social groups. It has been noted previously that 'being chosen' entails a need to conduct oneself in an orthodoxic and orthopraxic manner to maintain levels of 'chosen-ness'. In other words areas, behaviours, and beliefs that are not 'chosen' literally have the power to physically and symbolically 'pollute'. Foucault (1973) highlighted the point that boundaries operate to include and exclude, and that the more malign boundaries are not usually physical, but social and mental.

God's Way community maintain that their land is 'chosen' so that while on their community the physical environment, including the air they breathe, the food they grow and the water they drink, purifies them and helps nourish their sense of being 'chosen'. Their community is deliberately remote and several miles distance from their nearest neighbours; the only access roads are deliberately uneven to deter visitors. The entry to the community is strewn with wrecked vehicles and scrap metal to make it appear as if the community has been abandoned. The main living space is well hidden a few miles further down the track. This physical design is to deter visitors or other 'snoopers'. There is also a watchtower at the entrance gate which is also manned at night. Yet the fence that demarcates the community's land is low and wooden, in other words easy to traverse. The members do not monitor their boundary fence on a regular basis but instead believe that their 'rundown' design and their chosen' status will keep unwanted visitors out. The safety afforded them from the land's 'chosen' 'purity' is evidenced through a range of examples, including the fact that the dangerous wildlife that lived on or near the land, such as coyotes, wildcats and poisonous snakes, never attacked the members. They were believed to have been affected by the land's 'sacred' character to such an extent that it altered the animals' natural behaviour.

The community's members do not like leaving the community, even if it is to venture to the local town where most of the populace hold similar beliefs to themselves. On entry and exit to the community the members stop and say a prayer and take a drink from their communal well water, to help 'protect' their bodies. This ritual, in the Durkheimian (1915) sense separates and marks the division between sacred and profane space. The 'outside' is also controlled via the monitoring of media consumption; participation in external fundamentalist networks; and through rarely allowing anyone, but community members into the community. The discourse of 'purity' and 'pollution' is also commonly found in the wider fundamentalist community where Liberalism, Secularism and so forth are seen to 'pollute' individuals and communities alike. This can be seen in the drive to create fundamentalist alternatives to secular media, schooling, higher education, music, and so forth (Ammerman, 1991, Bruce, 2008, Harding 2000, Carpenter, 1997). These are particularly important for those communities who have to live in the secular world, for example in a city, and are unable to construct actual physical barriers to keep the secular world out.

The Role of Demonisation

'Othering' usually involves the demonisation of specific groups to support ideological or cultural beliefs of superiority (Arens, 1980, Said, 1978). Within this demonisation discourses of 'purity' and 'pollution' can predominate (Douglas, 1966, Arens, 1980). For example, homosexuals are not only seen as 'fallen' because they transgress Biblically decreed norms of sexuality and gender, but because their transgressive behaviour is seen to encourage diseases. This is viewed both as physical disease, such as AIDs or other sexually transmitted infections, which are deemed to have been 'created' and spread by homosexual promiscuity. But also 'spiritual' diseases that 'pollute' and 'corrupt' the 'soul', thus safe sex is deemed unsafe sex as it cannot protect the individual's soul from behaviour that is deemed 'wrong' in God's eyes. The demonisation of homosexuals also constructs a range of behaviours that homosexuals are seen as prone to, due to their 'base' depravity, such as, drug taking, alcoholism, paedophilia, rape of heterosexual men, and so forth. This form of demonisation can be seen in the literature of the 'Sexual Brokeness' movement as well as more general anti-gay campaigning among Protestant fundamentalists. Homosexuals are also identified as promoters of Liberalism, Secularism and anti-family values. They were seen by God's Way's members as having a hold on federal government where they were in a conspiracy with Jews, African Americans and Liberals.

In a similar vein African Americans were seen, by God's Way's members, as 'corrupted' both physically, mentally and spiritually. African Americans, like homosexuals, were seen as 'promoters' of disease through their perceived sexual promiscuity and lax morality, as exemplified, by the high rate of African American lone parent families. Similarly, like homosexual men, African American men were seen as rapists and 'corrupters' of morally 'pure' individuals. African Americans were seen as less intelligent than Whites and more prone to alcoholism and drug addiction. For God's Way community the 'proof' of this was the high rates of crime, poverty and drug addiction among African Americans in their home state. The community were against 'mixed marriage' and saw biracial children as 'wrong'. This meant that they were sympathetic to White supremacist activity that was rife in their region and saw it as 'putting Blacks back in their place'. The rise in visibility, and perceived socio-political influence of, both homosexuals and African Americans in the 1990s were interpreted by God's Way's members as a 'sign' that America was 'lost' to its 'true' citizens and that the end of the world must be near. Such demonisation was not applied to other categories of 'fallen', such as Catholics or Jews, which were disliked but not in the same virulent way. Finally, Liberals of any religico-cultural background were demonised as 'queers', 'drug addicts', 'promiscuous', 'un-American', 'Anti-Christian' and determined to promote Secularism and destroy the key institutions of American society from within, by taking control of education, government, business, the Arts and the media. This was the reason that God's Way community, in common with other fundamentalist Protestants, sought to promote their own parallel institutions and also gain political power where possible.

This particular demonisation of these three key categories of 'fallen' can be understood through the context of God's Way community specifically, and American protestant fundamentalism in the 1990s more generally. Firstly, God's

Way is situated in a state with high levels of racism that identified itself as part of the 'Old South', and thus has long-standing White animosity towards African American social progress and participation; therefore it is unsurprising that this group be singled out. Racism varies among Protestant fundamentalists in the USA, with higher levels in the southern states than the northern (Ammerman, 1991).

Homosexuals were demonised by God's Way because the 1990s was the decade when the American gay community became politicised in reaction to impact of the AIDs epidemic of the 1980s. The 1990s saw a greater call for equality, particularly in relation to marriage, and higher levels of visibility in the media. Homosexuality has always been deemed 'morally wrong' by fundamentalist Protestants among others, but it is only with a significant increase in gay political participation and visibility that this community have become so demonised. They serve as a useful target to focus fundamentalist campaigns on family, morality, children and sex education.

Finally, liberals have been the targets for fundamentalist anger and action since the late nineteenth century, indeed the emergence and rise of Liberalism was one of the causes of fundamentalism itself among American Protestants (Marsden, 1980). The post-Second World War politicisation of conservative Protestants was a reaction to the perceived progress of Liberalism across American society, institutions and government; and its perceived consequences of family breakdown, minority rights, economic decline, crime and 'immorality' (Ammerman, 1991, Bruce, 2008). In a sense Liberalism is a real, as well as symbolic, enemy to fundamentalist communities such as God's Way. After all Liberalism promotes cultural and moral relativism, secularism, freedom of speech, secular education, minority rights, gender equality and strives to avoid cultural chauvinism. In other words the values at the heart of Liberalism are the antithesis of the values and beliefs at the heart of religious fundamentalism.

Demonisation is a useful political strategy because it allows social groups to caricature specific individuals or groups to such an extent that they appear less than human and thus not worthy of sympathy or emotion. This makes it easier to campaign against such groups, and encourages often radical action; demonisation allows the group who demonise to deny commonalities and accentuate differences to such an extent that the demonised becomes non-human (Arens, 1980). This results in symbolic targets that operate to focus fundamentalist socio-political energies and action; thus offering a simplistic means to 'cure' social ills. For example, the targeting of homosexuals allows complex issues regarding sexuality, gender, moral plurality, family breakdown, minority rights, the role of the state to legislate the private domain, and the role of religion in secular society to be explored and 'solved' without having to engage in detailed and difficult socio-political discussions and dilemmas. Having already established 'demons' to target provides a shorthand and easily communicated political message with which to rally communities: everything that has gone wrong is the fault of the gays and if we can get rid of them our problems will cease. Isaac Zion summed up this view by saying 'if we killed all the fags it would be a start'. More mainstream

Protestant fundamentalist groups might not put it in such a way but might instead advocate 'curing' homosexuality, preventing equal rights for homosexuals or indeed criminalising homosexuality. The role of such key categories of 'fallen' in the political campaigns of fundamentalist Protestants will be explored in greater detail in the next chapter.

Chapter 8
'Fighting for God': The Politicisation of Fundamentalism

The final aspect of the fundamentalist worldview to be considered is that of its will to act in the world. The early interpretation of religious fundamentalism was of a movement of individuals and groups who could not cope with the consequences of modernity and therefore fundamentalism was seen to be reactionary at heart (Cole, 1931). This, perhaps, remains a stereotype (Bruce, 2008). However, religious fundamentalists are more revolutionary than reactionary; that is they seek to affect real socio-political change within their communities and countries. This is not a mere knee-jerk reaction to socio-cultural changes that they do not like, but rather a response to and a critique of those changes, accompanied with their own agenda for appropriate (that is in keeping with their own belief system) social change (Ammerman, 1991, Carpenter, 1997, Scott Jones, 2009). Their desire to act in the world is prompted and motivated by the other aspects of their worldview, particularly their sense of being 'chosen', which brings with it a unique sense of mission; and their belief in an imminent apocalypse, which results in a sense of immediacy and a desire to act in the present. The other aspects of their worldview, such as orthodoxy and orthopraxy, aid the reinforcement of their religious and political beliefs and aims, while facilitating the process of keeping followers 'on message'. The oppositionality of their worldview helps to construct 'ready-made' and easy to understand targets, for disaffection towards which political energies can be directed.

Possible Political Positions

Religious fundamentalists typically, adopt one of three political positions depending on the particular version of their belief system. The first is to adopt a 'retreatist position' whereby religious fundamentalist groups withdraw from mainstream society and thus any participation in social or political life. This approach is political if is supported by a critique of modern or late modern society, that identifies it as so corrupt that it is beyond redemption and thus to be left to face its apocalyptic fate. Groups, who take this approach, as God's Way community did in its early years, typically have two key features. First, they tend to view themselves as overwhelmingly 'chosen', above and beyond all other groups, however similar to them, and secondly, they have a strong sense of apocalyptic urgency which views the end of the world as literally imminent (Burkitt, 1914).

Retreatist groups by their nature tend to live in physical and social isolation from others and have a precarious existence in that they face a demographic dilemma in relation to recruitment. Perhaps, more seriously they have to confront the potential 'meaning crisis' event of failing to account for the lack of a predicted apocalyptic event (Festinger et al., 1964). Thus, such groups often have short life spans or fall apart following the death or departure of their founding, usually charismatic, leader (Kanter, 1972). God's Way community's shift from a retreatist, totally isolationist position was due to a demographic problem around recruitment and generational reproduction.

The second political position adopted by religious fundamentalists, particularly in the USA, has been what could be labelled as a 'gain a bridgehead' approach. This involves making small, but in the long term, significant gains within the political system, at city, regional, state or federal levels. The idea is that in gaining small 'bridgeheads' fundamentalist groups can then build support and gain greater influence. For example, by getting one of their candidates elected on to a local school board they can start to wield influence, perhaps cutting budgets to sex education programs or adding Creationism to the science curriculum.

This has been the key political strategy of Protestant fundamentalists, often in alliance with other conservative Christians, such as evangelicals, since the 1980s (Carpenter, 1997). This approach is based on the view that the system has the potential to be 'perfect' but needs to be 'saved' and reformed. This feeds into the American Protestant identity of being the 'true' Americans who created the original American democratic model in the first place (Wuthnow, 1989). In a sense their 'gain a bridgehead' approach is about 'taking back' what they see as their birthright that has been 'corrupted' (LaHaye, 1980). An example of this is in public education, where religious fundamentalists have campaigned hard to get their representatives on to school councils and city and state education boards with the power to actually put their issues on the agenda. This has been most successful in campaigns against sex education where ten states have adopted chastity and abstinence as the only approach to sex education; and in relation to the teaching of evolution where eight states now teach the Creationist account of life on Earth alongside the accepted scientific account.

The 'gain a bridgehead' strategy requires patience and sustained campaigning, along with the need for often substantial fund raising: all three qualities can be found in abundance in fundamentalist communities. This approach also means that small gains can be made at local or regional levels and provide communities with a sense of achievement with which to aim for the national stage. The key drawbacks of this approach are that they are time-consuming and usually require alliances to be made across denominational boundaries to gain strength in numbers and increase fund raising potential. Creating alliances is always problematic for fundamentalists as their view of being 'chosen' makes it difficult for them to cross the social and spiritual boundary that they maintain; in addition they find compromise challenging and that is often a key element in networking. The 'gain a bridgehead' strategy lends itself to democratic societies with freedom of speech and a free media, particularly those democracies with highly devolved decision making such as federal systems. These can be easily manipulated by minority campaigners.

The final political approach used by religious fundamentalists is that of 'regime change' or 'revolution'. This is most likely in societies which are not democratic and lack any structural apparatus, for example a free media, by which to affect socio-political change. This approach is fuelled by the view that the entire system is so 'corrupted' or 'immoral' that it must be completely over-turned and removed to be replaced by a theocratic style of polity. An example of this might be the Iranian Revolution of 1979. Fundamentalists who take this approach will usually utilise terrorist tactics to facilitate their struggle for change, although those targets might not directly be related to the institutions of state, but targets that will draw attention to their struggle. For example, Egyptian Islamic fundamentalists target western tourists as a means to publicise their political struggle and draw out confrontation with the Egyptian state. A similar tactic is used in Malaysia by Islamic fundamentalist groups (Bruce, 2008, Marty and Appleby, 1994). In the USA terrorism has not been a commonly used tactic of protestant fundamentalists who prefer, usually, to work within the democratic system. The main problem with taking a revolutionary approach to affecting socio-political change is that you threaten to alienate potential support within and outside of, your own community.

The Root of Politicisation

Religious fundamentalism is one of the best examples of the politicisation of religion. Karl Marx famously portrayed religion as a tool of oppression, 'the opium of the masses' that dulled the proletariat into submission and prevented them from seeing the 'real' version of reality. This view of religion as part of the mechanism of state oppression and a force of conservatism (rather than revolution) remained the mainstream interpretation of religion within the sociology of religion until the 1980s (McGuire, 1997). The increasing visibility of politicised religious fundamentalism in the Middle East and the USA aided a reinterpretation of long-standing views of the political potential of religious worldviews (Ammerman, 1991). The past three decades has seen religious fundamentalists in the USA and the Middle East, in particular, gain considerable political and cultural influence (Marty and Appleby, 1993a; 1995).

Fundamentalism among White Protestants in the USA, as has been noted, emerged in the latter half of the nineteenth century as a reaction to modernisation (Marsden, 1980). Initially, this reaction centred purely on theological issues, such as the position of Science, Scripture, literalism, and inerrancy in the modern world. Fundamentalism, with its stress on core values, moral Manichaeism, orthodoxy and Biblical literalism presented itself as a response, challenge and critique to Liberal and other forms of modernist Christian theology (Barr, 1977, Marsden, 1980). White, Protestant fundamentalists have an identity that entwines their religious and cultural identities, and so they believe themselves to be the 'true' or 'authentic' Americans and believers. Because of this fundamentalism quickly grew to encompass an increasingly sophisticated critique of modernity and the socio-cultural effects of modernisation upon American society (Wuthnow, 1989, Bruce, 2008). These effects, such as mass immigration, urbanisation and industrialisation were seen as threatening the way of life of the 'true' Americans, i.e. the White Protestants and of causing the 'moral' and thus social decline of the USA: a nation that White, Protestants view as a 'chosen' nation in itself with a global 'mission' to play. Thus political fundamentalism developed as a response to sweeping social changes (modernisation) and the perceived threat to cultural identity that those changes brought (Scott, 2001).

However Protestant fundamentalist participation in active, political and social campaigning did not really start until the 1970s. Before then fundamentalists focused their energies on spreading their beliefs among their different denominations and churches. Their ultimate aim was to 'push back' the spread of Liberalism within their own churches. The 'soul' of America was to be 'saved' by first halting the perceived decline of the 'true' religion (i.e. Protestantism) and then reinvigorating it with a 'back to basics' approach (i.e. fundamentalism) (Ammerman, 1991). In the 1920s, fundamentalists had worked with other conservative Christians to campaign against the teaching of evolution in public schools; a campaign that ended with the humiliation and ridicule that resulted from the Scopes 'Monkey' trial (Lienesch, 2007). This political failure coupled with the lack of success fundamentalists had in halting the rise of Liberalism, caused fundamentalists to regroup and focus on their own communities (Marsden, 1980). Fundamentalist communities started to build their own parallel social institutions, such as schools, colleges, media organisations and so forth. By the 1940s the issue of socio-political participation within the secular world was one of the key reasons behind the split between American evangelical and fundamentalist Protestants. The former seeing such participation as an important part of faith, the latter viewing such participation as unimportant for people with a greater 'chosen' mission (Marsden, 1980, 1984).

American protestant fundamentalism may have emerged in modernity, but it is in late modernity that it has become politicised. The 1950s and especially the 1960s saw a series of related socio-cultural changes occur in the USA that shifted it into a late modern society. Late modern societies privilege moral and cultural plurality; they are highly relativistic (Giddens, 1991). The so-called 'grand narratives' and therefore 'certainties' of modernity are dismantled and critiqued, such as Science, which opens the way, potentially, for religious revivals as individuals and communities face what might be characterised as 'existential homelessness' (Berger et al., 1973). Such societies are also highly individualistic and consumerist, which can be both liberating and alienating. Late modernity exacerbates the socio-cultural inequalities and problems of modernity, while removing the existential 'anchors' that modernity provided (Beck et al., 1994). For example, modernisation brought with it industrialisation, urbanisation and the rise in modern Capitalism.

All features which are potentially alienating and divisive. Yet, modernity also involved the creation of new communal identities that could provide a sense of social solidarity, for example, social class or nationality. Late modern society tends to see a decline in such providers of (potential) social solidarity (Beck et al., 1994). In this type of society the need for meaning and identity, typically, becomes an even greater issue than in modernity (Berger et al., 1973). Thus it should be no surprise that the era of substantial growth in religious fundamentalism around the world has been the late modern. Religious fundamentalism with its strong worldview and communal identity, coupled with a sense of divine mission, provides the perfect bulwark against the alienating effects of the late modern. But specific events provoke politicisation and this is certainly the case for the rise of political awareness among American protestant fundamentalists.

In 1963 the US Supreme Court outlawed prescribed prayers in public schools; this dismayed conservative Christians of all backgrounds as it seemed as if children were being told they could not pray in a nation which was established as a (White) Protestant utopia (Noll, 1992). However, at that time fundamentalists and many other conservative Christians did not see political participation as part of their religious worldview. The rest of the 1960s saw sweeping socio-cultural changes in the USA, culminating in 1973 with *Roe v. Wade* which legalised abortion. By the mid-1970s the USA had undergone dramatic and disorienting social changes, which radically disrupted and challenged a wide range of social institutions, such as the family. Long-established assumptions about race, sexuality, gender and identity were challenged and altered irrevocably. Events like the Vietnam War and Watergate seemed to suggest national decline both politically and morally. It is hardly surprising then that at this point fundamentalists and other conservative Protestants began to enter the political arena and offer an alternative vision for the USA (Ammerman, 1991).

Jerry Falwell, co-founder of the Moral Majority, identifies *Roe v. Wade* as the point when he began to wonder 'What can I do?' to help retrieve the 'soul' of America (Unger, 2005). The socio-economic decline of the USA in the 1970s and the failure of the Carter administration to either arrest that decline or put evangelical concerns at the centre of government policy, heightened fundamentalist fears and fuelled politicisation (Ammerman, 1991, Carpenter, 1997). This growing unease catalysed around the figure of Francis Schaeffer a Presbyterian evangelist and writer. Jerry Falwell identifies Schaeffer as his key influence and views him as the founder of the contemporary 'faith and values' movement (Unger, 2005). Schaeffer (1982) saw *Roe v. Wade* as the culmination of the 'moral decline' of the USA; a country that he now saw as sanctioning the 'murder' of unborn babies. Schaeffer (1982) criticised evangelical and fundamentalist Protestants alike; the former for their passive accommodation of the Secular-Humanist world, and the latter for their religious isolationism as America declined morally and socially. For Schaeffer, conservative Protestants had contributed to America's decline through their own political passivity. Schaeffer (1982) believed that conservative Protestants had a clear responsibility to engage in the secular world and 'fight back'.

Schaeffer's (1982) call to arms deeply influenced a range of Religious Right leaders, and Jerry Falwell in particular. Falwell, inspired by Schaeffer's (1982) call for action, sought out like-minded pastors willing to mobilise and politicise conservative Protestants, particularly fundamentalists (Unger, 2005). In 1979 Falwell met with Tim LaHaye, a right wing pastor from California. LaHaye had also been influenced by Schaeffer, and had put his words into action by founding Californians for Biblical Morality a coalition of conservative pastors who sought to fight on a range of social and moral issues across the state of California, including fighting against gay rights, for school prayer and even seeking to ban the game *Dungeons and Dragons* because it was deemed an 'occult' game. Falwell was impressed by the way that LaHaye had mobilised a network of like-minded pastors and churches to lobby the state government. LaHaye had utilised the 'gain a bridgehead' approach to good effect and had shown the potential power of grass-roots mobilisation of supporters. Seeing a model that might be applied on a national basis, Falwell, LaHaye and other fundamentalist leaders formed the Moral Majority, in 1979, an organisation that would seek to place fundamentalist issues at the heart of the nation and fight back against Secular-Humanism.

Falwell appealed to fundamentalists who might have preferred to remain in spiritual segregation by saying 'Only by godly leadership can America be put back on a divine course. God will give national healing if men and women pray and meet God's conditions' (Ammerman, 1991: 46). Their key campaign issues included supporting prayer and the teaching of Creationism in public schools; resisting gay rights legislation; repealing abortion legislation; and fighting against any Equal Rights Amendment (ERA). In his book, *The Battle for the Mind*, Tim LaHaye identifies Secular-Humanism as the source of social and moral decline in the USA. LaHaye, in common with most other prominent right-wing Protestant leaders, considers America's decline to be orchestrated by a coalition of Secular-Liberal-Humanists who actively seek to stamp out their White, Protestant way of life. LaHaye (1980) identified several key developments as evidence of this organised attack on this way of life, including a range of sex equality legislation that 'could be interpreted so as to prevent women fulfilling their biblical role as submissive wives'; the rise of gay civil rights; the ban on school prayer and the teaching to children of 'humanist' ideas, such as relativism 'that undermined the unwavering beliefs and traditions their parents held dear'; and the legalisation of abortion where 'the forces seeking to destroy traditional families and moral society seemed to converge in a court ruling that abortion was a matter of private choice' (cited in Ammerman, 1991: 40–41). LaHaye's easy depiction of a battle between 'good' (conservative Protestants) and 'evil' (Secular-Liberal-Humanists) was a simple way to identify complex social problems and offer solutions in a way that appealed to the apocalyptic beliefs and oppositional worldview of the majority of fundamentalists and evangelical Protestants. The 'othering' and demonisation discussed in the previous chapter aided the identification of political targets and facilitated this sense of 'good' versus 'evil'.

At the same time other conservative Protestant political organisations were being founded, including the American Coalition for Traditional Values, Christian Voice, and the Religious Roundtable. All had, at their heart, similar aims as the Moral Majority, and all appealed beyond their heartland areas of Protestant fundamentalism and evangelicalism but also attracted other types of religious conservatives (Bruce, 1988). However, the Moral Majority received the most media coverage and had the highest public profile; by 1980 the 'Moral Majority' had more than seven million members and its leaders worked hard to attract wealthy ultra-conservative donors (Ammerman, 1991, Bruce, 1988). The newly emerged and politicised 'New Christian Right' played a significant role in getting Ronald Reagan elected and in his re-election campaign Reagan actively courted the 'Religious Right'. The presidential campaigns of George H.W. Bush and especially of George W. Bush openly courted the 'Religious Right' (Ammerman, 1991, Unger, 2005); and groups like the Council for National Policy (CNP), a coalition of super-rich businessmen, fundamentalist pastors and right-wing tacticians worked to gain access to the highest levels of government. The extent to which significant victories were won by the politicised Protestant fundamentalists is open to much debate (Bruce, 1988, Carpenter, 1997, Ammerman, 1991). As is the extent of their populist appeal; clearly their viewpoints on some issues, such as abortion have a broad appeal to a wide range of voters beyond the fundamentalists and evangelicals, who offer the grassroots support for organisations such as the Moral Majority. In a sense the co-called 'Moral Majority' did not always speak for the 'majority' but on many issues they did manage to cross-religious and party lines (Bruce, 1988).

The Political Tools of Fundamentalism

Fundamentalism offers a range of political tools which have been utilised to great advantage by 'New Christian Right' organisations, such as the Moral Majority and the Religious Roundtable. Firstly, their sense of 'chosen' status, and therefore greater purpose, makes fundamentalists want to 'fight back' and 'fight for' (Marty and Appleby, 1991); this also makes them tenacious opponents as they believe that God is on their side and that they will ultimately triumph. Secondly, their apocalyptic beliefs lend a sense of urgency to any political fight; the clock is literally ticking. Apocalyptic beliefs can be tapped into, to provide ready-made 'enemies' to target (McGinn, 1994), as can their sense of oppositionality. Apocalyptic rhetoric lends weight to campaigning, whilst placing campaigns in a wider cosmic framework (McGinn, 1994). Thirdly, the strict behaviour and ethical codes of fundamentalists help provide a strong sense of identity, meaning and commitment that again can be used to rally communities and prove a bulwark against political disappointment (Scott Jones, 2009). Finally, their stress on community provides a ready-made supply of voters, campaigners and fund-raisers. Groups such as the Moral Majority particularly exploited points two and four to build their support, by tapping into already existing networks and communities of conservative Protestants. As was mentioned in previous chapters, Protestant fundamentalists had spent their political 'wilderness years' building their own parallel social institutions, including, publishing houses, television channels, schools, colleges, and so forth, and networks (Marsden, 1980, Carpenter, 1997). Such parallel institutions allowed easy channel for the dissemination of the political vision of the 'New Christian Right', whilst also providing easy to access, ready-made, networks of communities and churches to mobilise.

Indeed the importance of grass-roots campaigning has always been a key aspect of Protestant fundamentalist political action; with groups seeking to start at the local level and work up to the national level. This was the political model LaHaye (1980) had championed in California to good effect and which was quickly implemented across the nation. The political campaigning of American Protestant fundamentalists is a good example of the 'gaining a bridgehead' approach, whereby at local levels, churches and fundamentalist networks have encouraged their members to register for voting; to donate funds on key issues; to distribute campaign literature at a range of venues; to participate in local politics by getting elected on to health boards, school boards and local councils, and so forth. The existence of parallel fundamentalist institutions, particularly media ones such as television channels and now Internet sites, offer a ready-made stage for political issues to be presented, disseminated and debated.

The 'Culture Wars'

The term 'culture wars' was popularised by the sociologist James Davidson Hunter (1991), who used it to describe what he saw as a significant realignment and increasing polarisation, that was transforming American politics and culture. He argued that a range of socio-moral issues, including gun control, abortion, homosexual rights, censorship and the relationship between state and church, became increasingly high profile in the 1980s and especially by the early 1990s. These high profile issues exposed an American divide between opposing ideological worldviews, one which was progressive and liberal in nature and the other traditionalist and conservative. Although Hunter (1991) downplays the importance of religion within this ideological clash, the emergence of this conflict is directly linked to the politicisation of fundamentalist and other conservative Protestants in the early 1980s that placed socio-moral issues back at the centre of political debate. The nature of this clash was summed up by the ultra-conservative presidential candidate Pat Buchanan, in his now infamous 'Culture War' speech to the 1992 Republican National Convention in which he said 'there is a religious war going on in this country for the soul of America. It is a cultural war, as critical to the kind of nation we will one day be as was the Cold War itself.' In this speech Buchanan enunciated the 'New Christian Right's' view of what was 'wrong' with America and where this 'Culture War' was to be fought. He identified key battlegrounds as abortion legislation, gay rights, tax payer funded art and popular culture; stating that public morality was a central issue in 'saving' the nation (Jensen, 1995). Buchanan was reiterating the basic Protestant fundamentalist political vision. Buchanan failed to win the presidential election which saw the nation swing to the democrats under Bill Clinton, but his speech summarises the importance placed on public morality and popular culture during the political battles of this era.

Public morality is a key issue for fundamentalists, as well as other conservative Christians for a number of reasons. Firstly, is the view that the USA is a 'special' nation with a predestined divine 'mission' to lead the rest of the world. Therefore this nation founded by and on the values of White Protestantism must be 'saved' from moral corruption. This discourse has been a key element of the politicisation of protestant fundamentalists in the USA since the nineteenth century (Marsden, 1980). The federal or state funding of public art that is deemed offensive, for example the infamous (and tax payer funded) exhibitions of artists such as Mapplethorpe of the early 1990s, is not just offensive because it goes against long-held fundamentalist moral codes but also because it is seen as a symptom of a nation that is morally 'corrupted'.

The idea of a public consensus on moral issues is increasingly problematic in modern society as the division between the public and private sphere emerges (Bruce, 2002), and even more so in late modern societies, which tend to embrace cultural and therefore moral plurality on most issues (Giddens, 1991). This means that most western democracies tend to withdraw from legislating on the private moral conduct of individuals, for example, in relation to their sexuality, marital relationships and so forth, unless it relates to such activities that are almost universally viewed as morally repugnant, such as paedophilia or bestiality. The trend across the western world, of the past forty years, has been the liberalisation of family law and the decriminalisation of homosexuality. However, such a division between public life and private life is collapsed in fundamentalist communities; there is no separation, how one conducts oneself in public is how one must conduct oneself in private (Ammerman, 1993). Therefore fundamentalists and other conservative Protestants seek to remove the public/private divide and reintroduce moralising legislation, such as tougher divorce laws and the recriminalisation of homosexuality. In a sense then the private is as political as the public. The 'culture wars' was a means to 'play-out' this vision of a public morality in a populist, media friendly way.

Key Issues/Key Targets

The political campaigns of American protestant fundamentalists overwhelmingly focus on issues of public morality, family and the role of religion in public life (Bruce, 2008). Within those broad themes a number of key issues serve as the focus for politicisation and lie at the heart of campaigns. These key issues are as follows:

1. The Role of Religion in Public Life.
2. Abortion Legislation.
3. Homosexual Civil Rights.
4. The Decline of the Family.

1. Religion's Role in Public Life

Secularisation is an inevitable aspect of the modernisation of western societies and that results in religion moving from the centre of social life (and influence) to its margins (Bruce, 2002). Increasingly in modern societies, religion becomes an issue of personal choice and conscience. Western, democratic societies, like the USA, are built on Enlightenment values of individualism, freedom, equality and rationality; values that are antithetical to traditional religious worldviews. These values are supported and nurtured in the USA through the constitutional separation of religion and state (Berger, 1967, Bruce, 2002). For its first century as an independent nation, the USA was relatively homogenous as White and Protestant (Ahlstrom, 1975). Thus, even though there was a constitutional separation of religion and state this was not seen as problematic, as the nation's identity was seen as White and Protestant. The impact of modernisation began to disrupt this White Protestant hegemony, hence the initial emergence of Protestant fundamentalism (Marsden, 1980, Scott, 2001). However, it is in the post-war, late modern era that this hegemony is completely overturned, and direct challenges are made to the role of religion in public life, starting with the election in 1960 of John F. Kennedy, the first Catholic president, and accelerated by the successful 'social revolutions' of the 1960s.

The 1963 prohibition on prayer in public schools is often seen as the first step towards the politicisation of Protestant fundamentalists; and many fundamentalist leaders, such as Jerry Falwell view this as the start of their increasing unease with wider social change (Harding, 2000). Technically, prayer should be prohibited in American public schools in line with the Constitutional separation of church and state. However, this ban on prayer was interpreted by fundamentalists (and other conservative Christians) as a sign that the state had been taken over by the forces of Liberal-Secular-Humanism that sought to remove religion from public life. More than that, these forces were seen to be seeking to restrict 'public freedoms' of conscience and belief. Political resistance from fundamentalist and evangelical Protestants, to the ban on prayer was short lived and lacked the political networking of later fundamentalist campaigns. Attempts to revoke this legislation in the 1980s and Noughties have also failed. The failure to repeal the ban on school prayer led fundamentalists to focus their campaigning on issues that they are more likely to win due to their contentious nature, such as sex education, the teaching of the theory of evolution, and censorship, which will gain media attention and have the potential for wider public support.

Education is always a political battleground as it is a central social institution for inculcating key social values on to the next generation, what Tim LaHaye (1980) calls 'The Battle for the Mind'. As the majority of American children attend public schools; curriculum content can be an emotive issue for parents of all backgrounds. Fundamentalists targeted the teaching of sex education in public schools in the 1990s and Noughties. The teaching of sex education had begun to focus on a 'safe sex' message in response to the AIDs epidemic of the 1980s, and took an increasingly liberal approach to the subject, which de-emphasised the procreative nature of sex, publicised the availability of birth control and so forth. Fundamentalists and other conservative Christians were dismayed at what they deemed as such a 'liberal' approach that seemed to remove morality from the subject, and which went against their own particular view of sex, sexuality and procreation (Ammerman, 1993, Carpenter, 1997). Fundamentalists took three key political strategies, which were very successful; firstly, they promoted a legitimate alternative sex education, namely the promotion of chastity and abstinence, rather than just appear anti-sex education. This made the campaigns appear proactive rather than reactive, see for example, the educational materials produced by True Love Waits. Secondly, fundamentalists used their 'gain a bridgehead' approach extremely well by getting themselves elected on to local school, education and health boards at regional and state levels. By putting their own people into positions of influence and power, it then became easier to change curricula, direct funding and legislation. Thirdly, fundamentalists formed coalitions with other groups who supported their views, despite not being fundamentalists, such as Catholic groups and even the non-religious, such as conservative parents (Ammerman, 1991). Lastly, fundamentalist groups at all levels used negative media campaigning to get their message across, making sensationalist claims about the teaching of homosexuality and promiscuity in public schools (Harding, 2000). Media campaigns stressed how hard-earned tax dollars of 'decent' citizens were being used to promote 'free love' and 'deviant sex'. These campaigns throughout the Clinton era led to cuts to the funding of free clinics who distributed birth control, as well as to health promotion campaigns on 'safe sex'. By the Noughties, ten states had sex education curricula that focused solely on abstinence, and President George W. Bush offered federal funding to states that promoted abstinence-only sex education programs (Hauser, 2004). Organisation, networking, providing an alternative vision, and effective use of the media all proved highly successful. It would be used in a similar way to alter the science curricula.

The teaching of evolution in public schools first emerged as an issue in the 1920s and was the first political campaign in which Protestant fundamentalists took part. The failure of this campaign pushed fundamentalists out of the political arena for several decades (Lienesch, 2007). As their political power and confidence developed in the 1980s and 1990s, fundamentalist attention returned to the subject, but this time instead of being anti-evolution, campaigners provided an alternative vision: Creationism. By presenting Creationism as an alternative, quasi-scientific interpretation of the evolution of life, campaigners could avoid looking like anti-modern, flat-Earthers. Instead, they could support their claims with the dubious 'science' of Creationism; a good example of this attempt at proving intellectual worth is the 'work' of the Institute for Creation Science (ISR), which seeks to equip 'believers with evidence' (www.icr.org). The ICR even founded a museum, the now-titled Creation and Earth History Museum, located in Dallas, and run by the Life and Light Foundation. By presenting Creationism and its related theory of 'Intelligent Design', as theories competing with theory of Evolution to account for the origins of life on Earth, fundamentalists could present it as having scientific cache and weight. Creationism also plays on people's low levels of scientific literacy and on the wide acceptance of relativism in contemporary society (Numbers, 2006). The approach of getting their people elected on to education boards at all levels again allowed fundamentalist campaigners to alter science curricula or at least get Creationism taught alongside evolutionary theory (Numbers, 2006). By the mid-Noughties, eight states were teaching Creationism as part of the science curricula and in those states science textbooks on evolution carried a 'warning' sticker stating that evolution was a 'controversial theory some scientists present as a scientific explanation for the origin of living things ....No one was present when life first appeared on Earth. Therefore, any statement about life's origins should be considered as theory, not fact.' The children of God's Way community attended a local fundamentalist school, which did not teach any science and thus avoided the issue of evolution; the children were taught the Creationist view of Earth's origins. When they raised the issue of dinosaurs, which they had seen discussed on natural history programs on television, not being mentioned in the Bible, they were chastised and reminded that 'it was not their place to question God's word'.

The focus on education might seem strange given that a high percentage of fundamentalist children attend home schools or private faith schools. This can be partly explained by the fact that fundamentalists see the teaching of sex education and evolution, within the public school curricula, as evidence of a nation losing its religico-moral centre and coming under the grip of a conspiracy of Liberal-Secular-Humanists. The battle for abstinence-only based sex education and the teaching of Creationism/ 'Intelligent Design' in the classroom, was partly about taking the 'fight' to those forces that fundamentalists see as actively 'corrupting' the nation and trying to wipe out Christianity in the USA. They are also both issues that can have broad public appeal and support.

A final way that fundamentalists have tried to challenge the decline in religion's role in public life has been through the issue of taxpayer funding to the Arts. Fundamentalists have long seen the art world as dominated by Liberal-Secularists who use the arts to promote their 'immoral' message (Harding, 2000). The greater political awareness of fundamentalists, by the late 1980s, helped ignite the 'culture wars' (Hunter, 1992) that used the Arts and popular culture as a forum for disseminating their vision of an America 'gone astray', and their critique of the state as morally 'corrupt'. Again, by getting their members elected on to local councils they could actively work to ban art exhibitions or cut funding to 'immoral' art projects. The late modern world of the Arts in the 1990s, with its bent for sensationalism and shock, provided fuel for fundamentalists' campaigns that suggested that contemporary artists promulgate 'pornography' and 'anti-American' messages. Using the media to good effect, fundamentalists could raise the issue of taxpayer dollars being misused. Much of this 'culture war' centred around issues of freedom of speech and censorship, which meant that in the long-term fundamentalists were doomed to lose the battle as the art world had the Constitution on their side (Bruce, 2008). However, the war on the world of the Arts could be used to support their other political campaigns.

2. Abortion Legislation

The legalisation of abortion was the catalyst for the mobilisation of fundamentalists in the 1970s, when leaders like Schaeffer, LaHaye and Falwell saw the state sanctioned 'murder' of the unborn as evidence of a country that had lost its 'soul' (Unger, 2005, Luker, 1984). Abortion is a key issue not just, because it is seen as 'murder' of a 'gift' from God, but also because it potentially empowers women, while removing rights from men; and because it potentially may be seen as encouraging sexual experimentation and promiscuity. This issue also had broad appeal beyond the world of fundamentalists, providing an opportunity for greater political networking (Guth et al., 1993). Again, fundamentalists made good use of the media to promote the Pro-life stance, evoking images of the Holocaust. Abortion was used to enunciate a powerful critique of capitalism (through the figure of rich doctors profiting from 'murder'), the modern state (that sanctions such 'murder'), and feminism (which empowers women to 'kill' their babies) (Luker, 1984). The prohibition of abortion was presented as a key step to 'saving' the soul of the nation (Harding, 2000, Ammerman, 1991). Fundamentalists worked together in networks, utilising a range of political strategies. By using their 'gain a bridgehead' approach, they got their representatives elected to local councils and health boards so that they could cut public funding to abortion clinics. They lobbied local and state politicians, often using extreme techniques such as sending aborted foetuses to Pro-choice candidates. Campaigners also took direct local action by picketing clinics, trying to stop women and staff from entering them. Some groups vandalised clinics, while others publicised local doctors who conducted abortions, by leaving placards outside their houses 'naming and shaming' them (Carpenter, 1997, Ammerman, 1991). Finally, a minority took more militant action by attacking clinic staff and buildings, resulting in many deaths. The most famous and coordinated abortion campaign was Operation Rescue, which started in 1988 (www.operationrescue.org). Their basic approach was to blockade clinics; holding prayer vigils, and pleading with women and staff not to enter. When clinics won court orders, against the protestors, they refused to leave and hundreds were arrested. Such militant action was not necessarily condoned by all fundamentalist leaders but these tactics did succeed in putting abortion at the heart of political debate in the 1990s (Ammerman, 1991, Ginsburg, 1993, Mouw and Sobel, 2001). God's Way community worked in alliance with other groups, including a local Catholic group, to picket the one abortion clinic in their area and they took turns holding vigils outside it. God's Way's community's members also regularly took part in leafleting the local community with emotive pro-life pamphlets that featured pictures of aborted foetuses and the names and addresses of clinic staff. Their most militant action, which they often discussed with great pride, was to spray pig's blood over the front lawn of a local doctor who they believed to be conducting abortions. They had been participating in such campaigning since the 1980s. However, again Protestant fundamentalists and their allies failed to overturn long-standing legislation and abortion remains legal in the USA.

3. Homosexual Civil Rights

While abortion emerged as a key political battleground in the 1980s, homosexuality has become a key battleground of the late 1990s and into the Noughties. Although fundamentalists have always been against homosexuality as it violates Biblical codes relating to gender and sexuality, it has not been a political issue until more recently. This was due to the criminalisation of homosexual sex and the invisibility of the gay community. This changed in the early 1990s with the politicisation of the gay community in response to the AIDs epidemic of the 1980s (Gallagher and Bull, 1996), evidenced by the emergence of organisations such as the Human Rights Campaign (HRC), and the Gay and Lesbian Alliance Against Defamation (GLAAD). By the 1990s, the gay community was demanding greater civil rights and equality in the areas of taxation, housing, employment and marriage. The Clinton administration enacted a series of sexual orientation equality laws, culminating in the overturning of the ban on gays serving in the military (Gallagher and Bull, 1996). This improvement in gay civil rights was accompanied by increasingly normalised depictions of gays in popular culture, for example, the hit late 1990s sitcom *Will and Grace* featured two gay characters as leads. By the Noughties, the issue of gay marriage has become increasingly prominent, as the USA remains out of step with nearly all other western democracies in not permitting some form of homosexual civil union. For fundamentalists increasing gay civil rights and the seeming normalisation of homosexuality is deeply troubling and reinforces their view that the nation is in the grip of Liberal, Secular-Humanists, hell-bent on 'moral corruption' (Gallagher and Bull, 1996). As discussed in the previous chapter, homosexuals also provide useful targets that can be heavily demonised as promiscuous hedonists, with paedophiliac tendencies, and a propensity to spread disease. The 'gay marriage' debates of the past decade have provided a useful vehicle for fundamentalists and other conservative Christians to promote their own political agenda. Gay marriage is not seen as problematic just because it involves greater rights for homosexuals, but because it represents the normalisation of homosexuality and its equalisation in relation to heterosexual marriage. Fundamentalists have played on widespread homophobia and fears about the decline of the family to block or overturn gay marriage rights in several states, most recently in California in 2008. Fundamentalists have used their usual grassroots strategies of building alliances with other interested parties, mobilising voters within their own constituents, raising substantial campaign funds, lobbying state government, and making good use of emotive and sensationalised media messages. When these have failed, fundamentalists have picketed gay 'weddings'. The notorious Westboro Baptist church pickets the funeral of servicemen killed in Iraq and Afghanistan to protest against gay marriage and the 'fag lifestyle of soul-damning, nation-destroying filth'; bearing placards that scream 'fags must die' and 'God Hates the USA' (see www.godhatesfags.com). However that sort of protesting is seen by the majority of Protestant fundamentalists as 'immoral' in itself as it violate the funerals of American soldiers, who are seen as the ultimate patriots.

4. The Decline of the Family

The perceived decline of the 'traditional' American family and the view that the state is trying to dismantle and attack this family is at the heart of most Protestant fundamentalist campaigns. The 'traditional' family is defined, of course, as a unit of two married, heterosexual parents and their children. In this definition, the father works to support his family and the mother is the homemaker (Ammerman, 1993, Bendroth, 1994). This definition is the way in which fundamentalists view the family and see all deviations from this model as morally wrong. The decline of the family is evidenced by fundamentalists, through America's high divorce and illegitimacy rates; the promotion of gay marriage rights; high levels of child abuse and abortion; high rates of sexually transmitted diseases; and high levels of lone parent families. A wide range of social ills are seen as consequences of the decline in the traditional family, for example, high rates of truancy, crime, drug abuse, mental illness, delinquency, and so forth (Harding, 2000, Carpenter, 1997). For fundamentalists the 'traditional' family is 'God-given' and its roles divinely sanctioned. To create alternative family forms or to attack the 'traditional' family is seen by fundamentalists as going against God's will and therefore the 'natural' order of things (Bendroth, 1994, Marty and Appleby, 1993b). The moral and spiritual 'health' of the nation cannot be improved unless the 'traditional' family is supported and protected (Lahaye, 1980). Thus, family issues are at the heart of all fundamentalist political campaigns and they facilitate exploration of widespread social changes involving the family, gender, and sexuality (Bendroth, 1994, Marty and Appleby, 1993b). Again, campaigns on family issues can allow them to access wider political alliances and networks outside of their core constituencies.

Family issue campaigns utilise the same political strategies as other campaigns, including 'gaining a bridgehead' into local and state decision making; using the media; mobilising grassroots supporters (and voters); and raising campaign funds. Fundamentalist campaigns on family issues of the past thirty years are prompted by three central concerns; firstly, a desire to protect the 'traditional' family and thus prevent the normalisation of alternative forms (Lahaye, 1980, Bendroth, 1994, Marty and Appleby, 1993b). Thus they campaign against gay marriage and gay adoption rights; the extension of welfare to lone parents; public funding of shelters for abused women and helplines for abused children. Secondly, they are concerned with protecting women's roles as homemakers and wives by stopping legislation that normalises and facilitates the working mother (Ammerman, 1993). Finally, there is a concern to protect men's status as leaders, protectors and providers.

Fundamentalists are concerned with what they perceive as the marginalisation of men and a deliberate agenda of feminisation of society and government, for which they blame feminists, Liberals and Secularists. They have successfully blocked all attempts to pass the ERA and they campaign against the extension of maternity employment rights and the provision of paternity leave (Boone, 1989, Marty and Appleby, 1993b, Ammerman, 1991, Unger, 2005). At a local level fundamentalist campaign to block public funding to shelters for abused women; day-care centres for working women; and birth control clinics.

The campaign for the family has also been fought out in the media. Tim LaHaye's wife, Beverly, founded Concerned Women for America (CWA) to oppose the 'anti-marriage, anti-children, anti-man feminism' (Unger, 2005: 144) that she saw promulgated through organisations like the National Organization for Women (NOW) and federal government itself. The organisation's website (www.cwfa. org) has become a powerful publicity tool and forum for promoting pro-family campaigns; a central aspect of which has been to target popular cultural depictions of 'alternative' family forms. They also organise boycotts of networks and sponsors of television shows that promote what they perceive to be an 'anti-family', 'anti-male' agenda. A recent example was their targeting of the successful network show *Desperate Housewives,* which was seen to glamorise adultery, working wives (and mothers), weak husbands, and gay marriage. Such media campaigns have been piecemeal in their success, as they require support from outside of conservative religious constituents and go against widespread consensus support for gender equality.

Where fundamentalists have been successful in gaining support for their family campaigning has been in focusing less on the religious reasons for protecting the family and more on the issue of government intervention in family life. This ploy has been successful in tapping into long-standing American anxieties about the extension of the powers of the state (Harding, 2000, Bruce, 2008). Thus, debates about extending parental employment rights become less about whether the state should or should not support working parents, and more about the extent to which the state should be involved in the decisions individuals make about their family and working lives.

Common Interests

One aspect of fundamentalist political campaigning has been the creation of alliances with non-fundamentalists, including groups who might be seen as 'heretical' by most fundamentalists, such as Catholics (Ammerman, 1991). Following their split with evangelicals in the 1940s, fundamentalist Protestants had focused inward and avoided working with those they deemed to be 'non-believers' (Barr, 1977, Marsden, 1980). However, by the 1970s there was an increasing awareness, promoted by leaders such as Francis Schaeffer (1982) that like-minded Christians should work together on common interests. This led organisations like the Moral

Majority to work alongside non-fundamentalists on many campaign issues where there was a shared common ground. Leaders like Jerry Falwell acknowledged that this meant working within and by secular rules (Ammerman, 1991). This led to some rather odd alliances, for example, fundamentalist and evangelical groups campaigned alongside feminist groups on the issue of pornography, yet were on opposing sides on the issue of abortion and women's rights (Bendroth, 1994). Fundamentalists worked with Catholics on pro-life campaigns and Mormons on opposing the ERA. Many fundamentalists saw this as pragmatic politics where the ultimate political goals were worthy of the sacrifice of communal exclusivity (Ammerman, 1991). God's Way community campaigned alongside local churches and faith groups on issues such as abortion and gun control, without seeing it as a 'contamination' of their belief system. Isaac Zion, the current leader of God's Way, saw it as a necessity when 'our foes are so strong and wicked'.

However, some fundamentalist leaders, for example, Bob Jones, saw such networking as morally and spiritually wrong. Jones and others saw spiritual and social separation as key to fundamentalist belief and identity. After all, the issue of participation in secular society had been at the centre of the post-war split between fundamentalists and evangelicals (Barr, 1977, Marsden, 1980). They saw such separation as critical to the fundamentalist way of life and their ultimate apocalyptic destiny. They shared a view that participation in the secular world of politics risked 'contaminating' fundamentalist communities and jeopardising their spiritual destiny. Leaders like Falwell and LaHaye responded to such criticism by stressing the overwhelming sense of urgency to 'save' America and by tapping into long-standing foundation myths of a 'chosen' nation founded by a 'chosen' people (Unger, 2005, Ammerman, 1991). This approach seemed to be effective.

Evaluating Success

The extent to whether Protestant fundamentalist and other conservative Protestant groups have actually been successful at changing legislation to suit their political agenda is open to debate (Ammerman, 1991, Carpenter, 1997, Bruce, 2008). None of the Republican presidents of the past thirty years of 'New Christian Right' campaigning have enacted legislation of great significance to fundamentalists and evangelicals; for example, abortion is still legal, women's and gays' rights legislation continues apace with other western democracies. Religion remains separate from the state as enshrined in the Constitution. The polarisation of the 'red' and 'blue' states is not as marked as 'culture wars' theorists might present (Koch and Steelman, 2009). However, lobbying by conservative Protestants has managed to suffocate any attempt to pass the ERA for the past three decades and encouraged the enactment of the *Marriage Protection Act* in 2007.

Nevertheless, fundamentalist Protestant political campaigning, alongside evangelicals and other conservative Christians, has made a difference politically on three levels. Firstly, they have been politically successful in terms of getting their agenda enshrined in legislation and policy, at regional and state levels, particularly in traditionally conservative states. Secondly, through their work at creating the climate for and then fuelling the so-called 'culture wars' (Hunter, 1992), in which opinion on social and moral issues has become increasingly polarised and confrontational, has meant that such issues are now at the centre of cultural (and political) debate. Finally, and in relation to the last point, in seeking to put social and moral issues at the centre of cultural debate, Protestant fundamentalists have managed to attract the political sympathies of a broad range of people who would not classify themselves as fundamentalists or evangelicals, but who are anti-abortion and anti-gay marriage. The politicisation of American fundamentalists and evangelicals has led to the current cultural-political climate in the USA where moral issues, such as gay marriage and abortion, have much greater political weight than in most comparable western countries. The fight for the moral 'soul' of the nation is still ongoing.

Chapter 9
'Taking it to the World': Fundamentalism in a Global Context

The modern era's birth in the eighteenth century had been the end product of a series of cultural and political revolutions, for example, the Renaissance, the Reformation, the French and American Revolutions, and the Industrial Revolution (Calinicos, 2007, Evans, 2006). Enlightenment thinkers took the idea of the modern, and defined and valorised it. Modernity was to be the era where Science, rationality, logic and empiricism would triumph; alongside democracy, justice and (objective) 'truth'. Religion was associated with the traditional, superstitious, undemocratic, past; a 'relic' to be challenged and removed from modern society. This view of religion profoundly influenced classical social science theorists who presented religion (specifically Christianity) as anti-modern, reactionary, conservative, and concerned with preserving the status quo. This viewpoint forms the basis of what would develop into the Secularisation Thesis (Bruce, 2002), with its basic contention that as societies modernise religion 'loses its social significance' (Wilson, 1966). Although this theory has since been modified to acknowledge the European specificity of the model (Davie, 2002, Bruce, 2002), it remains dominant in sociology and other social sciences, with its central idea that Modernity and modernisation has a profound impact, typically detrimental, on religious cultures and communities. This view that modernisation negatively impacts on religious cultures influenced the early theorists of religious fundamentalism (for example, Cole, 1931), who, typically, presented such fundamentalism as a 'knee jerk' reaction to modernity. This view led sociologists (and others) to ignore the phenomenon of religious fundamentalism as an emerging socio-political force in the world. Hence, as Ammerman notes (1991), the surprise in 1976, within academic, media and political circles, of the election of President Carter, partly through the bloc voting of conservative Protestants; as well as the events of the Iranian Revolution of 1979 that ushered in the world's first Islamic fundamentalist state. Soon the word 'fundamentalist', with its roots in early American protestant fundamentalism, entered popular usage and was applied (not always accurately) to a wide-range of religico-political groups and movements (Scott Jones, 2009).

As this book has discussed, the shift into modernity, ironically, has been the catalyst for the emergence of religious fundamentalism in the USA and beyond. Rather than cause religious believers to adopt a retreatist position, modernisation has provoked mobilisation and politicisation (Marsden, 1980, Wuthnow, 1989), which has been accelerated in the late modern era (Giddens, 1991, Scott, 2001). Chapter 8 explored the nature of Protestant fundamentalist political campaigning;

demonstrating the highly effective political strategies utilised by protestant fundamentalists and other conservative Christians in the USA. The desire to act in the secular world is a key component of their worldview; although the extent of political action varies across communities and groups. Religious fundamentalists in the USA, and elsewhere, may appear to be 'anti-modern' with their critiques of modernity, but in fact they are communities that make the most of the modern, while presenting an alternative to it.

An Alternative Modernity

American protestant fundamentalists invoke images of a 'golden age' of protestant dominance in America, when the nation was homogenous, rural, traditional, and to an extent pre-modern (Harding, 2000, Ammerman, 1991). This is mere socio-political rhetoric, using the past to lend historical legitimacy and weight to their political campaigns. Although, as discussed previously in this book, Protestant fundamentalists' sense of religico-cultural identity is linked to ideas of being a 'chosen' people who founded a 'chosen' nation (Ahlstrom, 1975, Scott, 2001); contemporary protestant fundamentalists have no real intention of recreating a mythical past. They work to remake the present to conform to their values and beliefs. These are communities that seek to reshape modern society to their own ends; in other words they present an alternative vision of modernity.

The impact of modernity upon Christianity specifically and then American society, generally, at the end of the nineteenth century provoked a 'back to basics' movement that became what we now identify as 'fundamentalism' among White Protestants. By the end of the nineteenth century, White, Protestants in the USA had enjoyed over a century of cultural and religious hegemony (Ahlstrom, 1975); they were not an obviously marginalised or oppressed community. One might not expect a socio-political movement to emerge from within this group.

Religious fundamentalism emerges in communities that have three central aspects; firstly, a communal identity that entwines religion with an ethnic or national identity. Secondly, that community perceives (real or imagined) this identity to be 'under threat' in some way, whether that be through social or political marginalisation, oppression, conquest, and so on. Thirdly, this 'identity threat' is set against a backdrop of wider (and often rapid) socio-political changes within a region or nation that marks a shift into and often an embracing of modernity. Modernity being problematic as it not only triggers a series of processes of modernisation that profoundly alter the structure of societies; specifically secularising forces that challenge religion's position within that structure. For example, White, American protestant fundamentalists have a religico-national identity that presents themselves as 'true' or 'authentic' Americans (Scott, 2001). Initially they experienced identity 'threat' through real attacks on religion's position within a modernising society; as demonstrated by the rise to prominence in the nineteenth century of theological Liberalism, which encouraged an end to Biblical Literalism and expounded the values of Biblical Criticism (Barr, 1977, Marsden, 1980). This theological modernising caused White, conservative Protestants to begin to coalesce around a critique of such modernising, that invoked a sense of getting 'back to the basics' of faith; in other words adhering to the view that a reiteration of the 'fundamentals' would reinforce and strengthen religion's position in mainstream society (Marsden, 1980, Ammerman, 1991). At the same time, wider social changes were occurring in American society that started to make White, protestants believe that their identity (and long-standing hegemonic authority) was 'under threat' from the incumbent processes of modernisation, including, mass immigration, urbanisation, industrialisation and so forth. In hegemonic terms, White, protestants suffered no real loss of socio-political power at this time; but the perception of 'threat' was sufficient to motivate action. Initially then, religious fundamentalism can appear to be a reactive movement, provoked by rapid social changes, causing individuals to retreat into the existential safety of religion (Berger, 1967). However, if this was the case fundamentalists would not involve themselves in socio-political activities and instead retreat into isolation, avoiding contact with secular society. Only a minority of fundamentalist groups take the retreatist approach; most seek to effect social change (Ammerman, 1991, Carpenter, 1997, Bruce, 2008)

Instead, religious fundamentalist movements seek to provide resistance to one version of modernity, whilst offering an alternative vision of how modernity might be. White, Protestant fundamentalists in the USA offer resistance to the dominant version of modernity that privileges secularism, privatism, moral and cultural plurality, individualism, consumerism, and increasingly interventionist government. This version of modernity is seen as socially and morally 'wrong'; the evidence of which is seen in a wide range of social problems, including family breakdown, immigration, rising levels of crime and welfare dependency, child abuse, high levels of alcohol and drug dependency, and so forth (Bruce, 2008, Ammerman, 1991, Unger, 2005). It is also evidenced through what are perceived to be 'attacks' on American culture in the media, popular culture, and the Arts (Hunter, 1992). For Protestant fundamentalists, American society is 'broken', morally 'corrupt' and not worthy of its 'chosen' nation status. The identification of social problems as evidence of a 'corrupt' society serves to prove two things; firstly, when people stray too far from the morally 'correct' way of living, i.e. the Protestant fundamentalist way, then they start to live their lives in ways that are detrimental to themselves and society at large. Secondly, such 'immorality' encourages the spread of 'UnAmerican' sentiments and a decline in patriotism, which allows the media and popular culture to broadcast unpatriotic values, ideas and to promote 'UnAmerican' ideas.

Because Protestant fundamentalism is a revolutionary movement rather than a reactionary one, it not only offers a critique of what is wrong with contemporary society, but also puts forward an alternative vision for living. This vision places religious values, specifically, those of conservative Protestantism, at the centre of socio-cultural and political life (LaHaye, 1980). In this vision of society, morality would cease to be a 'private' matter and would become a public and political issue; thus government would once again legislate on moral issues, such as abortion, homosexuality, divorce, pornography, and so forth. Religious values would be embedded in social institutions, such as schools, universities and media organisations. This vision does not entail taking apart the existing political structures of the American state; Protestant fundamentalists are pro-democracy and support the Constitution. Indeed, conservative (White) Protestants consider themselves to be the descendants of the founders of American democracy (Ahlstrom, 1975, Scott, 2001). Rather, the fundamentalist vision for America is to remove from power and influence those forces that they identify as causing the shift away from 'true' values, namely the forces of Secularism, Liberalism, and Humanism (LaHaye, 1980). Replacing these forces with the religious values of conservative Protestantism is viewed as the 'solution'. By restoring the hegemonic authority of White, Protestants, the 'chosen' people of the 'chosen' nation; the USA will go through a period of social, political and moral renewal (LaHaye, 1980, Wuthnow, 1989, Harding, 2000).

Fundamentalism's ability to offer both critique and a 'solution' through an alternative vision, make it a radical socio-political force in the USA and elsewhere. The core elements of the fundamentalist worldview feed this radicalism. The core belief in being 'chosen' allows individuals and communities to believe that God is on their side and has selected them to do 'his work'. The belief that they hold in a forthcoming apocalypse lends agency and urgency to their political activities; as well as framing them with a greater cosmic meaning (Scott Jones, 2009, McGinn, 1994). Their strict codes for living and believing reinforce meaning and communal identity, while their oppositionality allows the construction and demonisation of specific political targets (for example, homosexuals, Jews, Liberals, feminists, etc.) with which to channel their campaigning energies. All of these elements work together, to push fundamentalists to act in the world in order to facilitate social and political change.

Making the Most of the Modern

Marty and Appleby (1991) make the point that religious fundamentalists are highly selective in relation to what aspects of modern life they will critique. They may invoke images of the past and seem to reiterate a return to it; but this is all rhetoric. Indeed religious fundamentalists are contradictory in their relationship towards modern life; on the one hand they criticise it and yet they make good use of most of what modern life has to offer. For example, Protestant fundamentalists might identify the Internet as the potential arena for the Anti-Christ and a place where their 'enemies' promulgate their 'immorality'. Yet, the Internet has become a key media for the dissemination of fundamentalist messages and the mobilisation of communities. Fundamentalists may not acknowledge this but they are a by-product of modernisation; and modern and indeed late modern society allows them to create the alternative society that they seek. American Protestant fundamentalists, typically, embrace the technologies, wealth, consumerism, and other advantages of modern life. Such advantages have allowed them to build their own parallel institutions, such as universities, hospitals, schools, theme parks, museums, record labels, publishing houses and so forth. These institutions serve to maintain a sense of communal identity; establish 'safe' spaces for their communities, which are free of potentially 'corrupting influences; socialise the next generation of fundamentalists into the faith; and serve to provide alternative models for secular institutions They may be awaiting the forthcoming 'Rapture' but they do so by making the most of the modern, particularly in relation to using the tools of secular modernity against itself.

What about the Rest of the 'Family'?

The fundamentalist worldview presented in this book is applicable across White, Protestant fundamentalists in the USA. But it should be stressed that contextualising all groups is essential and there will be variation as to the degree of commitment to some elements of this particular worldview. For example, some protestant fundamentalists will work in alliance with non-fundamentalists for the pragmatic accomplishment of political goals. The Moral Majority and God's Way community both adopted this strategy; but such pragmatism has been viewed as 'morally wrong' by other Protestant fundamentalists, for example, Bob Jones, who sees separatism as crucially important and not something that can be compromised. Similarly, God's Way community stress that they alone are uniquely 'chosen' by God, albeit with some ambiguity with regard to their fellow fundamentalists; whereas many other fundamentalists would see this as too exclusive a claim.

This book has focused on the worldview of White, Protestant, fundamentalists in the USA, but to what extent is this form of fundamentalism similar to that of other types of religious fundamentalism in other parts of the world. This book adopted the 'family resemblances' approach to fundamentalism (Marty and Appleby, 1991: ix–x) which proposes a unitary definition of religious fundamentalism. Chapter 2 discussed the debate surrounding the use of unitary definitions and these will not be revisited here. Suffice to note that although they propose a unitary definition of fundamentalism, Marty and Appleby (1991), also stress the importance of contextualising all fundamentalist groups, historically, geographically, and culturally. That said the conditions that provoked religious fundamentalism among White, Protestants in the USA can be found to have a similar causal effect across the globe. Specifically, we can identify the three conditions outlined earlier in this chapter, namely:

1. A pre-existing, strong, religico-ethnic/national identity.
2. A sense of political, cultural, economic, or social 'threat'; real or imagined.

3. The 'identity threat' that operates is contextualised within wider (and often rapid) socio-political changes, which represent a move towards modernity.

This can be seen in a range of fundamentalisms, across different religions and regions.

Islamic Fundamentalism

Islamic fundamentalism, alongside Protestant fundamentalism in the USA, is the most significant form of fundamentalism in the world today. It emerged in the early decades of the twentieth century. Islamic fundamentalism in the Middle East emerged first in Turkey in the 1920s. Under the leadership of Mustafa Kemal Ataturk, the newly independent Turkey was established as a secular nation. Ataturk embarked on a program of deliberate 'modernisation', which sought to take Turkey into modernity. This program was wide reaching and involved a range of reforms, including ending gender segregation, adopting the Latin alphabet, prohibiting traditional dress and encouraging western style clothes, banning religious symbols from state institutions, and so forth (Ahmad, 1993). This program equated modernisation with westernisation and secularism. These reforms occurred within a decade, which is a short period of time for any form of significant social change. Islamic fundamentalism emerged as a response to this, with many Turks feeling their intertwined identity as Muslims/Turks was under threat. That threat was identified as westernisation and secularism; both of which appeared to shift Islamic practice to the margins of society. Although Turkey remains a secular state there still exists a tension between the secular, modern vision of Turkey and fundamentalists who reiterate an Islamic vision of modernity for Turkey (Cleveland, 2004).

In a similar vein in Iran in the post-Second World War era, the Shah, Mohammad Reza Shah Pahlavi, embarked on a program of modernising and westernising. Iran underwent rapid industrialisation and urbanisation, in the 1950s and 1960s, as oil reserves were exploited. This created greater social divides and concentrated poverty in urban centres. The Shah's 'westernisation' program included, ending gender segregation, banning the veil, giving women the vote, promoting education, and limiting the power of religion, specifically Islam (Daniel, 2001). Although industrialisation produced a consumer society, with a growing middle class; those Iranians who did not benefit from the 'Shah's revolution' felt that their sense of identity as Iranians/Muslims was 'under threat' (Cleveland, 2004). As in Turkey, Islamic fundamentalism emerged in response to these changes, culminating in the overthrow of the Shah and the establishment of an Islamic fundamentalist state. In newly-independent Egypt, in the 1950s, President Nasser, also promoted a deliberate program of modernisation and westernisation (Cleveland, 2004). As with Iran, this created a more unequal society. Nasser saw westernisation as synonymous with progress and economic development, groups like the Muslim Brotherhood reacted to Nasser's modernisation efforts by asserting a specific pan-Arab, Islamic agenda that reinforced communalism and a strong religious and cultural identity. Islamic fundamentalism remains a disruptive force in Egypt where increasing social inequalities and a repressive state apparatus ensure its growth.

In South East Asia, Islamic fundamentalism emerged and remains a problem in Indonesia and Malaysia; again in response to rapid industrialisation and modernisation in the 1970s and 1980s (Marty and Appleby, 1994). Islamic fundamentalism is a socio-political force across the Middle East, in parts of South East Asia, and across former Soviet republics in central Asia. It emerges in those areas where an identity as a Muslim is embedded within an ethnic or national identity. This identity is perceived to be 'threatened', and sometimes in the case of repressive regimes this can be a reality. This sense of 'threat' occurs during social and economic changes which are identified as 'modern'. But this version of the modern is viewed as western and therefore 'unIslamic', which further intensifies the perception of 'identity threat'. This becomes particularly sensitised in those regions which were once governed by western colonial powers (Marty and Appleby, 1994). The lack of democratic structures and institutions in many Middle Eastern and Asian states facilitates the growth of religious fundamentalism by establishing mosques as the only forum for political dissent and debate; therefore channelling dissent through religion.

Other Types of Religious Fundamentalism

Israel and India were both established as secular states. But following independence fundamentalist groups started to emerge. Israel was founded as a secular state, albeit with a strong Jewish cultural identity. There has always existed a tension between the secular and the religious; Israel's system of proportional representation produces coalition governments that rely on minority parties. This provides Jewish fundamentalists, through voting for ultra-right wing parties, with access to political decision-making particularly in relation to the conflict with the Palestinians. After Israel's victory in the 'Six Days' War', Jewish fundamentalist groups emerged who saw the Israeli victory as a sign that 'Greater Israel' was to be reinstated. They started building 'settler' communities across the occupied West Bank. Groups like Gush Emunim have become increasingly militant as Israel participates in peace talks with the Palestinians (Bruce, 2008). Thus in Israel Jewish fundamentalism relates to a sense of dissatisfaction with secularism and modernism. The sense of 'threat' and the context of social change relates to Israel's tense relationship with neighbouring Arab states and with the Palestinians.

Secularism was also one of the defining features of an independent India; but Hindu fundamentalist groups soon emerged, post-independence, that sought to establish 'Hindutva' a Hindu state. Such groups target Muslim and Christian communities, and support those politicians who seek to stall attempts to find a solution to the Kashmir 'problem' (Marty and Appleby, 1994). As India emerges as a key global economic power, increasing numbers of Indians are being left out of India's 'economic miracle' and it is likely that many will be drawn to Hindu fundamentalism which asserts a Hindu/Indian identity, which sees non-Hindus and secularism as their 'identity threat'.

Globalisation and Religious Fundamentalism

Globalisation is an accelerant to the growth of religious fundamentalism in late modernity (Scott Jones, 2009). Globalising forces make the world increasingly interlinked and interdependent; culturally, economically and politically (Hall 1992, Turner, 1991). Globalisation speeds up the effects of economic modernisation, making communities more economically vulnerable. The nation-state becomes increasingly powerless to control transnational corporations (TNCs), for example, Nike and Microsoft, whose economic power often brings with it potential political power, since a state's refusal to accommodate a TNC, could lead that corporation to move its operations elsewhere, with an obvious detrimental economic effect. Thus, nation-states can appear politically weak in the face of a globalised economy, which can, in turn, make communities seek alternative political models (Hall, 1992). Additionally, global trends in politics can make communities feel marginalised in the shift toward an interconnected global polity, which is perceived as a form of Western hegemony. The seeming resistance to democratisation in the Middle East, for example, could be interpreted as a resistance to a Western model being imposed upon communities who already feel besieged culturally. Islamic fundamentalists present visions of purely Islamic states that offer an alternative political model, which also draws on a pre-existing cultural heritage. (Scott Jones, 2009).

An increasingly globalised media allows the promotion of alternative visions to be shared across communities and regions. Satellite broadcasting and the Internet are key avenues for resistance and for the promotion of alternatives, as can be seen in their widespread use by Islamic fundamentalists across the globe and Protestant fundamentalists in the USA (Scott Jones, 2009). Globalisation is taken to symbolise a shift toward a uniform global culture typically considered 'Western' and specifically 'American'. This shift inevitably creates the need for cultural resistance, which may be achieved through the stressing of 'authentic' versions of cultural identity (Hall 1992, Turner, 1991). Fundamentalists are particularly adept at making claims to 'authenticity'; drawing on their sense of 'being chosen' as evidence that theirs is the 'true' belief/identity. In a non-Western context, globalisation has a profound impact, amplifying the effects of modernisation and creating the ideal conditions for the emergence of fundamentalism (Scott Jones, 2009, Marty and Appleby 1994, 1995).

In the Western context, globalisation creates a range of socio-economic conditions, including greater economic insecurity; a questioning of sociopolitical structures; greater consumer, cultural, and political choice; and encourages cultural plurality. Globalisation's impact in the West is to provoke debates around identity and values, which can lead some individuals to seek out alternatives.

An example of this would be the growth of Islamic fundamentalism in the United Kingdom, among young, British-born Asians (Scott Jones, 2009). In accommodating cultural plurality, some communities may feel 'under threat', as demonstrated by the growth of fundamentalism among White Protestants in the USA (Bruce, 2008). When that sense of threat is combined with the economic insecurity globalisation inevitably brings, then communities can be plunged into 'meaning crisis'; such a situation can make religious fundamentalism an attractive 'solution'.

Religious fundamentalism provides a complete 'meaning package', making it an attractive socio-political movement to counter the uncomfortable 'meaning flux' facing numerous communities around the world. This 'meaning package' involves a number of features. Firstly, it asserts the importance of religion, which is appealing in itself to communities, with religico-ethnic identities, who feel 'under threat'; since religion is familiar to them and is highly effective at protecting against 'meaning crisis' (Berger, 1967). Secondly, fundamentalism asserts that the fundamentalist has been 'chosen' by God and therefore has a special relationship with God. When mixed with apocalyptic rhetoric portraying fundamentalists as doing God's work and on a fixed time scale, the assertion gives life instant meaning. The oppositionality and separatism of fundamentalism also works to reduce the impact of competing meaning systems, and thus allows the individual to restore meaning, by eradicating the potential existential confusion of 'choice'. Finally, fundamentalism offers of a specific critique of (modern) society and an agenda for socio-political change that allows the fundamentalist to see the 'bigger picture' and understand why life is bad now, but also how it will change in the future and improve. Fundamentalism is, overwhelmingly optimistic in its view of change, asserting that change, when it comes, will be for the better because fundamentalists are doing 'God's work' and if it is 'God's work', then it must be for the better (Scott Jones, 2009).

Ultimately, the appeal of fundamentalism is security in a deeply insecure world. Security can be taken to mean in a psychological, socio-political, or economic sense. Proof of the strength of this worldview to provide meaning and security is evident in the high levels of optimism and confidence found among many fundamentalist groups; typically, religious believers score highly on tests for positive mental attitudes, but fundamentalists test even higher (Clark and Lelkes, 2009, Hackney and Sanders, 2003, Altemeyer, 2003). So psychologically, the fundamentalist worldview and way of life, are highly effective in making people feel contentment, happiness and confidence. But security can also refer to socio-political and economic security (Scott Jones, 2009). Fundamentalism offers a critique of what is wrong with a specific nation or community, and provides a strategy for change. It identifies specific political targets and often offers a time frame, influenced by apocalyptic beliefs. Fundamentalists have a strong sense of security and righteousness because they believe that theirs is 'God's work' and that God is one their side (Marty and Appleby, 1991). Religious fundamentalism will continue to be a growing force for change and resistance, in the twenty first century, because it offers a powerful response to modernisation and globalisation (Bruce, 2009, Marty and Appleby, 1994, 1995), which specifically resonates with communities who do not view secularisation as an inevitable aspect of the shift into modernity (Scott Jones, 2009, Bruce, 1008).

Fundamentalism's Futures

The growth of religious fundamentalism caught the social sciences, political commentators, and the media by surprise (Ammerman, 1991). Although there has been an increase in theoretical and empirical studies of religious fundamentalism (see for example the work of Marty and Appleby, 1991, 1993a, 1993b, 1994, 1995), much of the work remains ignored by social policy and political analysts. Despite the increased incidence of terrorist attacks around the world that have links to religious fundamentalism; and the role fundamentalism plays in fuelling many contemporary conflicts, across the world, there remains a lack of 'joined-up' analysis where social science research informs and shapes government policy and diplomacy.

The fundamentalist worldview, as this book has argued, is very specifically constructed and directly informs action; action cannot be understood, or predicted, unless the construction of worldview is studied within its specific socio-cultural context. To illustrate, the 7/7 London bombers were British born Muslims, many from affluent, university-educated backgrounds: they did not fit the stereotype of the disaffected, poor, and marginalised terrorist. In the past terrorist organisations, such as the IRA, used to issue coded warnings ahead of attacks and the bombers themselves were usually far from danger. Contrast that approach with the proliferation of suicide bombings and the distinct lack of any attempt to warn potential victims; interview transcripts with imprisoned failed suicide bombers attest to their lack of empathy with potential victims. The rules have changed, and so a more informed and 'joined-up' approach needs to be taken to deal with the emergence and growth of religious fundamentalism, particularly the varieties that adopt terrorist tactics (Scott Jones, 2009).

The factors that tend to provoke religious fundamentalism as a socio-political force have been understood for some time within social science research (Marty and Appleby, 1991 and 1994, Ammerman, 1991, Bruce, 2008), and yet these studies do not seem to inform foreign or social policy. The increasingly dire security situation in Iraq and Afghanistan, are examples of where the growth of religious fundamentalism and its role in destabilisation, could have been predicted and therefore actions could have been taken to counteract its effects. As globalisation and modernisation continue to affect different communities around the world, religious fundamentalism will continue to grow as a form of resistance; providing an alternative vision of how the world could be. Indeed, globalisation will further accelerate fundamentalist action, particularly given the increasing shift toward a globalised politics and through the increasingly, pervasive global media. As the world becomes ever more interconnected, the message and actions of fundamentalists can be easily and quickly spread; allowing them to influence similar groups. An example of this would be the role of the media, particularly the Internet, and the increased availability of cheaper air travel in spreading Islamic fundamentalism, from the Middle East to Europe.

The continued growth of religious fundamentalism poses a range of serious security and socio-political issues. The oppositional and separatist aspects of fundamentalism create a feedback loop that can, potentially, escalate fundamentalist actions: the need to construct and demonise 'enemies' and targets increases tensions with the wider secular community, while the oppositionalism of fundamentalists makes it harder for them to seek compromise (Scott Jones, 2009). As outsiders react to fundamentalists' actions, fundamentalists take this as further proof of the righteousness of their cause and become ever more hard-line and extreme. The rules of negotiation and political compromise become much more problematic when dealing with fundamentalists, who believe that they are 'right' and that those who are not 'chosen' by God are lesser in every way and, most important of all, part of the problem in the first place. Religious fundamentalism can be reduced in the non-western world, but doing that requires new ways of dealing with global issues. This might involve dealing with the issue of Western-supported repressive regimes in the Middle East and elsewhere; finding ways to bring about more effective economic redistribution and aid to developing nations; encouraging the development of indigenous systems of political participation that speak to people's cultural heritage; and the formulation of foreign policy approaches that resolve key territorial conflicts that fuel disaffection. All of these would be examples of ways to tackle the growth in religious fundamentalism around the non-western world.

Religious fundamentalism in the western context is unlikely to decline. Late modern society, with its existential 'homelessness' (Berger et al., 1973); moral and cultural plurality; cultural ennui; consumer culture; and eclecticism, offers a positive environment for the growth of religious fundamentalism. The uncertainties of culture, identity, consumption, belief and so forth (Beck et al., 1994) that characterise our age mean that there will always be individuals who seek out the security of certainty. Fundamentalism is highly effective at providing both existential security and certainty. As Tipton (1984) found in his study of counter-culturalists; facing endless uncertainty and choice can be spiritually and mentally exhausting, driving many in his study to the certainties of fundamentalist and other conservative forms of belief. Similarly, late modern society offers many avenues for fundamentalists to gain a socio-political forum. For example, moral and cultural plurality necessitates endless rewriting of equality and human rights legislation; such legislation can then be exploited by fundamentalists. For example, in the UK recent equalities legislation was passed that limited freedom of speech in relation to the defamation of religious groups. The fundamentalist group Christian Voice used this to attempt to shut down performances of *Jerry Springer: The Musical*; they failed but the case has highlighted the potential misuse of this legislation to prohibit freedom of speech. In a similar vein the debate about Creationism has spread from the USA into Europe, partly because relativism has become so dominant that increasingly public opinion is being swayed against Evolution and towards Creationism (Dawkins, 2006). Fundamentalists are becoming increasingly canny about using the forces of Liberalism against itself. Protestant and Islamic fundamentalism in the western world has led to an increasing polarisation in political and cultural opinions (Hunter, 1992); but more importantly it has led to the re-emergence of religion as a political force. A force that, throughout the Noughties in Europe and the USA, has provoked new debates concerning the extent and limits of democratic structures and freedoms, particularly on issues relating to freedom of speech, minority rights, and the role of religion in education. It would seem that not only has religious fundamentalism found its socio-political place within the late modern world, but also is finding it a beneficial environment for its continued growth and success.

Bibliography

Ahlstrom, S.E. 1975. *A Religious History of the American People, Volume One*. Garden City, NY: Doubleday Image Books.

Ahmad, F. 1992. *The Making of Modern Turkey*. London: Routledge.

Altemeyer, B. and Hunsberger, B. 1992. Authoritarianism, religious fundamentalism, quest, and prejudice. *International Journal for the Psychology of Religion*, 2, 113–33.

Altemeyer, B. 2003. Why do religious fundamentalists tend to be prejudiced? *The International Journal for the Psychology of Religion*, 13, 17–28.

Ammerman, N.T. 1991. North American Protestant Fundamentalism, in *Fundamentalisms Observed*, edited by M.E. Marty and R.S. Appleby. Chicago, IL: University of Chicago Press, 1–65.

Ammerman, N.T. 1993. *Bible Believers: Fundamentalists in the Modern World*. New Brunswick, NJ: Rutgers University Press.

Arens, W. 1980. *The Man-Eating Myth: Anthropology and Anthrophagy*. Oxford: Oxford University Press.

Asch, S.E. 1955. Opinions and Social Pressure. *Scientific American*, 193, 111–37.

Barr, J. 1977. *Fundamentalism*. London: SCM Press.

Beck, U., Giddens, A., and Lash, S. 1994. *Reflexive Modernization: Politics, Tradition and Aesthetics in the Modern Social Order*. Oxford: Blackwell Publishers.

Bellah, R.N. 1967. Civil religion in America. *Daedalus,* 96, 1–21.

Bendroth, M.L. 1994. *Fundamentalism and Gender: 1875 to the Present*. New Haven, CT: Yale University Press.

Berger, P.L. 1967. *The Sacred Canopy: Elements of a Sociological Theory of Religion*. Garden City, NY: Doubleday.

Berger, P.L. 1999. The Desecularization of the World: A Global Overview, in *The Desecularization of the World: Resurgent Religion and World Politics*, edited by P.L. Berger. Grand Rapids, MI: W.B. Eerdmans Publishing Company, 1–18.

Berger, P.L., Berger, B., and Kellner, H. 1973. *The Homeless Mind: Modernization and Consciousness*. New York, NY: Random House.

Berger, P.L., and Luckmann, T. 1966. *The Social Construction of Reality: A Treatise in the Sociology of Knowledge*. Harmondsworth: Penguin.

Bloch, E. 1985. *Visionary Republic: Millennial Themes in American Thought, 1750–1800*. Cambridge: Cambridge University Press.

Boone, K.C. 1989. *The Bible Tells Them So*. Albany, NY: State University of New York Press.

Boyer, P. 1992. *When Time Shall Be No More: Prophecy Belief in Contemporary American Culture*. Cambridge, MA: The Belknap Press of Harvard University Press.

Bruce, S. 1988. *The Rise and Fall of the New Christian Right*. Oxford: Oxford University Press.

Bruce, S. 1990. Modernity and fundamentalism: the New Christian Right in America. *British Journal of Sociology*, 41 (4), 477–96.

Bruce, S. (ed.) 2001. *Religion and Modernization: Sociologists and Historians Debate the Secularization Thesis*. Oxford: Oxford University Press.

Bruce, S. 2002. *God is Dead: Secularization in the West*. Oxford: Blackwell Publishers.

Bruce, S. 2008. *Fundamentalism*. Cambridge: Polity Press.

Burkitt, F.C. (1914). *Jewish and Christian Apocalypses*. London: The British Academy, Oxford University Press.

Callinicos, A. 2007. *Social Theory*. Oxford: Blackwell Publishers.

Carpenter, J.A. 1997. *Revive Us Again: The Rewawakening of American Fundamentalism*. New York, NY: Oxford University Press.

Clark, A.E. and Lelkes, O. 2009. Let us pray: religious interactions in life satisfaction. *PSE Working Papers 2009–10*, PSE (Ecole normale supérieure).

Cleveland, W.L. 2004. *A History of the Modern Middle East*. Boulder, CO: Westview Press.

Cohen, S. 1972. *Folk Devils and Moral Panics*. Oxford: Blackwell Publishers.

Coles, S.G. 1931. *The History of Fundamentalism*. Hamden, CN: Archon Books.

Connell, R.W. 1995. *Masculinities*. Cambridge: Polity Press.

Connell, R.W. 2002. *Gender*. Cambridge: Polity Press.

Daniel, E.L. 2001. *The History of Iran*. London: Greenwood Press.

Davie, G. 1994. *Religion in Britain since 1945: Believing without Belonging*. Oxford: Blackwell Publishers.

Davie, G. 2002. *Europe: the Exceptional Case. Parameters of Faith in the Modern World*. London: Darton, Longman and Todd.

Dawkins, R. 2006. *The God Delusion*. London: Bantam Press.

Dollar, G.W. 1973. *A History of American Fundamentalism*. New York, NY: Random House.

Douglas, M. 1966. *Purity and Danger: An Analysis of Concept of Pollution and Taboo*. London: Routledge.

Doyle, L. 1999. *The Surrendered Wife*. London: Simon & Schuster.

Durkheim, E. 1915. *The Elementary Forms of Religious Life*. Oxford: Oxford University Press.

Durkheim, E. 1989. *Suicide: A Study in Sociology*. London: Routledge.

Eliade, M. 1963. *Myth and Reality*. London: George Allen and Unwin Ltd.

Elias, J.L. 1999. *Islam*. London: Routledge.

Ellinson, C.G. 1996. Conservative Protestantism and the Corporal Punishment of Children: Clarifying the Issues. *Journal for the Scientific Study of Religion*, 35 (1): 1–16.

Evans, M. 2006. *A Short History of Society: The Making of the Modern World*. Maidenhead: Open University Press.

Festinger, L., Riecken, H.W. and Schachter, S. 1964. *When Prophecy Fails*. New York, NY: Harper & Row.

Foucault, M. 1973. *The Birth of the Clinic: An Archaeology of Medical Perception*. London: Tavistock.

Foucault, M. 1979. *Discipline and Punish*. Harmondsworth: Penguin.

Gallagher, J., and Bull, C. 1996. *Perfect Enemies: The Religious Right, the Gay Movement, and the Politics of the 1990s*. New York, NY: Crown Publishers.

Gallup, G., and O'Connell, G. 1986. *Who Do Americans Say I Am?* Philadelphia, PA: Westminster Press.

Gallup, G., and Castelli, J. 1989. *The People's Religion: American Faith in the '90s*. New York, NY: Macmillan.

Gallup. 2008. 'Church Attendance Stable despite Tough Times', (published 17 December 2008) <www.gallup.com>, accessed 14 May 2009.

Gallup. 2009. 'Church-Going Among U.S. Catholics Slides to Tie Protestants', (published 9 April 2009) <www.gallup.com>, accessed 12 April 2009.

Geertz, C. 1966. Religion as a Cultural System, in *Anthropological Approaches to the Study of Religion*, edited by M. Banton. London: Tavistock.

Gerth, H.H., and Mills, C.W. (eds). 1991. *From Max Weber: Essays in Sociology*. London: Routledge.

Gibson, C.J., and Lennon, E. 1999. Historical Census Statistics on the Foreign-born Population of the United States: 1850–1990. *Population Division Working Paper 29*. Washington, DC: US Census Bureau.

Giddens, A. 1991. *The Consequences of Modernity*. Stanford, CA: Stanford University Press.

Gilsenan, M. 1990. *Recognizing Islam: Religion and Society in the Modern Middle East*. London: I.B. Tauris.

Ginsburg, F. 1993. Saving America's souls: Operation rescue's crusade against abortion, in *Fundamentalisms and the State*, edited by M.E. Marty and R.S. Appleby. Chicago, IL: University of Chicago Press.

Gupta, D. 1993. Between general and particular 'others': some observations on fundamentalism. *Contributions to Indian Sociology* (n.s.), 27 (1), 119–37.

Guth, J.L., Schmidt, C.E., Kellsdelt, L.A., and Green, J.C. 1993. The Sources of Anti-Abortion Attitudes: The Case of Religious Political Activists. *American Politics Quarterly* 21(1): 65–80.

Hackney, C.H. and Sanders, G.S. 2003. Religiosity and Mental Health: A Meta-analysis of Recent Studies. *Journal for the Scientific Study of Religion*, 42(1): 43–55.

Hall, S. 1992. *Formations of Modernity*. Cambridge: Polity Press.

Harding, S.F. 2000. *The Book of Jerry Falwell: Fundamentalist Language and Politics*. Princeton, NJ: Princeton University Press.

Hauser, D. 2004. Five Years of Abstinence-only-until-Marriage Education: Assessing the Impact. *Advocates for Youth* <www.adocatesforyouth.org>, accessed 18 October 2007.

Hechter, M. 1987. *Principles of Group Solidarity*. Berkeley: University of California Press.

Heelas, P. 1997. *The New Age Movement*. Oxford: Blackwell Publishers.

Herberg, W. 1956. *Protestant, Catholic, Jew*. Garden City, NY: Doubleday.

Hervieu-Leger, D. 2000. *Religion as a Chain of Memory*. Cambridge: Polity Press.

Hunsberger, B. 1995. Religion and prejudice: The role of religious fundamentalism, quest, and right-wing authoritarianism. *Journal of Social Issues*, 51, 113–29.

Hunsberger, B. 1996. Religious fundamentalism, right-wing authoritarianism, and hostility towards homosexuals in non-Christian religious groups. *The International Journal for the Psychology of Religion*, 6, 39–49.

Hunter, J.D. 1992. *Culture Wars: The Struggle to Define America*. New York, NY: Basic Books.

Jensen, R. 1995. The Culture Wars, 1965–1995: A Historian's Map. *Journal of Social History*, 29, 17–37.

Kanter, R.M. 1972. *Commitment and Community*. Cambridge, MA: Harvard University Press.

Kanter, R.M. (ed.), 1973. *Communes: Creating and Managing the Collective Life*. New York, NY: Harper & Row Publishers.

Kaplan, J. 2006. Islamophobia in America? September 11 and Islamophobic Hate Crime, *Terrorism and Political Violence*, 18 (1), 1–33.

Knight, P. 2000. *Conspiracy Culture – American Paranoia From the Kennedy Assassination to The X-Files*. London: Routledge.

Koch, P.R., and Steelman, L.C. 2009. From Molehills Mountains Made: An Examination of Red and Blue State Cultural Stereotypes. *Cultural Sociology*, 3 (1), 165–89.

LaCayo, R. 1999. The End of the World As We Know It? *Time*. 18 January 1999.

LaHaye, T. 1980. *Battle for the Mind*. Ada, MI: Fleming H. Revell.

LaHaye, T. and LaHaye, B. 1998. *The Act of Marriage: The Beauty of Sexual Love*. Grand Rapids, MI: Zondervan.

Lawrence, B. 1989. *Defenders of God*. San Francisco, CA: Harper & Row.

Laythe, B., Finkel, D.G., and Kirkpatrick, L.A. 2001. Predicting Prejudice from religious Fundamentalism and Right-Wing Authoritarianism: A Multiple Regression Approach, *Journal for the Scientific Study of Religion*, 40 (1), 1–10.

Laythe, B., Finkel, D.G., Bringle, R.G., and Kirkpatrick, L.A. 2002. Religious Fundamentalism as a Predictor of Prejudice: A Two-Component Model. *Journal for the Scientific Study of Religion*, 41 (4), 623–35.

Lienesch, M. 2007. *In the Beginning: Fundamentalism, the Scopes Trial and the Making of the Anti-evolution Movement*. Chapel Hill, NC: University of North Carolina Press.

Lindberg, C. 2005. *A Brief History of Christianity*. Oxford: Blackwell Publishers.

Luker, K. 1984. *Abortion and the Politics of Motherhood*. Berkeley, CA: University of California Press.

Lukes, S. 1985. *Emile Durkheim: His Life and Work, a Historical and Critical Study*. Stanford, CA: Stanford University Press.

Marsden, G.M. 1980. *Fundamentalism and American Culture: The Shaping of Twentieth Century Evangelicalism 1870–1925*. New York, NY: Oxford University Press.

Marsden, G.M. 1984. *Evangelicalism and Modern American Culture*. New York, NY: Oxford University Press.

Martin, D. 2005. *On Secularization: Towards a General Theory*. Aldershot: Ashgate.

Marty, M.E., and Appleby, R.S. (eds). 1991. *Fundamentalisms Observed*. Chicago, IL: University of Chicago Press.

Marty, M.E., and Appleby, R.S. (eds). 1993a. *Fundamentalisms and the State*. Chicago, IL: University of Chicago Press.

Marty, M.E., and Appleby, R.S. (eds). 1993b. *Fundamentalisms and Society*. Chicago, IL: University of Chicago Press.

Marty, M.E., and Appleby, R.S. (eds). 1994. *Accounting for Fundamentalisms*. Chicago, IL: University of Chicago Press.

Marty, M.E., and Appleby, R.S. (eds). 1995. *Fundamentalisms Comprehended*. Chicago, IL: University of Chicago Press.

Marx, K. 1990. *Capital: A Critique of Political Economy*. Harmondsworth: Penguin.

McGinn, B. 1979. *Visions of the End: Apocalyptic Traditions in the Middle Ages*. New York, NY: Columbia University Press.

McGinn, B. 1984. *Apocalypticism in the Western Tradition*. Aldershot: Variorum.

McGuire, M.B. 1997. *Religion: The Social Context*. London: Wadsworth.

Mouw, T., and Sobel, M.E. 2001. Culture Wars and Opinion Polarization: The Case of Abortion, *American Journal of Sociology* 106(4): 913–43

Munson, H. 1995. Not all crustaceans are crabs: reflections on the comparative study of fundamentalism and politics. *Contention*, 4 (3), 151–66.

Noll, M.A. 1992. *A History of Christianity in the USA and Canada*. London: SPCK.

Numbers, R. 2006. *The Creationists: From Scientific Creationism to Intelligent Design*. Cambridge, MA: Harvard University Press.

Plutzer, E., and Berkman, M. 2008. Trends, Evolution, Creationism, and the Teaching of Human Origins in Schools. *Public Opinion Quarterly*, 72: 540–53.

Rabinow, P. 1984. *The Foucault Reader*. New York, NY: Random House.

Runnymede Trust. 1997. *Islamophobia: a challenge for us all: report of the Runnymede Trust Commission on British Muslims and Islamophobia*. London: Runnymede Trust.

Ruthven, M. 1989. *The Divine Supermarket: Travels in Search of the Soul of America*. London: Chatto and Windus.

Said, E.W. 1978. *Orientalism*. New York, NY: Random House.

Salehi, M.M. 1998. *Insurgency Through Culture and Religion: The Islamic Revolution of Iran*. London: Praeger.

Sandeen, E.R. 1970. *The Roots of Fundamentalism: British and American Millenarianism 1800–1930*. Chicago, IL: University of Chicago Press.

Schaeffer, F. 1982. *A Christian Manifesto*. Wheaton, IL: Crossway Books.

Scott, J.F. 1996. *Unfinished Sympathy: Embodiment of Faith in an American Fundamentalist Christian Intentional Community*, unpublished PhD thesis, University of Edinburgh.

Scott, J.F. 2001. 'You and Me Against the World': Christian Fundamentalists and White Poverty in the USA, in *Globalization and National Identities: Crisis or Opportunity?* edited by P. Kennedy and C. Danks, 80–96. London: Palgrave.

Scott Jones, J. 2009. Fundamentalism, in *Globalization and Security: Social and Cultural Aspects*, edited by G.H. Fagan and R. Munck, 136–51. Santa Barbara, CA: Praeger Security International.

Sennett, R. 1996. *The Fall of Public Man*. New York, NY: W.W. Norton.

Ter Haar, G. 2003. Religious fundamentalism and social change: a comparative inquiry, in *The Freedom To Do God's Will: Religious Fundamentalism and Social Change*, edited by G. Ter Haar and J.J. Busuttil. London: Routledge.

Tipton, S. 1984. *Getting Saved from the Sixties*. Berkeley, CA: University of California Press.

Turner, B.S. 1991. *Religion and Social Theory*. London: Heinemann.

Unger, C. 2005. American Rapture. *Vanity Fair*, December 2005.

Weber, M. 1991. The social psychology of the world religions, in *From Max Weber: Essays in Sociology*, edited by H. Gerth and C.W. Mills. London: Routledge.

Weber, M. 1992. *The Protestant Ethic and the Spirit of Capitalism*. London: Routledge.

Weeks, J. 1989. *Sexuality*. London: Routledge.

Wiesner, M.E. 2000. *Christianity and Sexuality in the Early Modern World: Regulating Desire, Reforming Practice*. London: Routledge.

Wilson, B.R. 1966. *Religion in Secular Society*. London: C.A. Walker.

Wuthnow, R. 1989. *The Struggle for America's Soul: Evangelicals, Liberals, and Secularism*. Grand Rapids, MI: Eerdmans

Index